Praise for Reframe Your Viewpoints

"Virginia Ritterbusch's non-fiction motivational self-help book, *Reframe Your Viewpoints: Harness Stress & Anxiety—Transform It Into Peace & Confidence*—is an inspiring and informative work ... She presents real-life scenarios to enable a fuller understanding of the topics covered... Through this process, one can actively change one's perspective on life and create a positive outlook from the inner stress and anxiety triggered by events and other sources ... I was immediately fascinated by the material she presents on the brain and how reframing can actually change the way the brain responds to stress and stressors, and I loved the way she broke down what could be a complex subject into more accessible parts, using helpful examples and reinforcement. Ritterbusch's experience and educational background are obvious in her command of the subject, as well as her most helpful use and citation of referential texts and motivational quotes. Her writing style is conversational, and reading through her book makes you feel as though she's in the room, discussing the eight strategies directly with you. I also appreciated how she offered alternative approaches to enable the reader to personalize their experience. *Reframe Your Viewpoints* is most highly recommended."

Jack Magnus
Readers' Favorite

REFRAME YOUR VIEWPOINTS

**Harness Stress & Anxiety
Transform It Into Peace & Confidence**

VIRGINIA RITTERBUSCH

Publisher's Cataloging-in-Publication Data
provided by Five Rainbows Cataloging Services

Names: Ritterbusch, Virginia.

Title: Reframe your viewpoints : harness stress & anxiety, transform it
    into peace & confidence / Virginia Ritterbusch.

Description: Orlando, FL : Life Changes Publishing House, 2018.

Identifiers: LCCN 2018902031 | ISBN 978-0692-13838-0

Subjects: LCSH: Reframing (Psychotherapy) | Cognitive therapy.
    | Neurolinguistic programming. | Acceptance and commitment
    therapy. | Mindfulness-based cognitive therapy. | Empathy. |
    BISAC: SELF-HELP / Neuro-Linguistic Programming (NLP) |
    PSYCHOLOGY / Movements / Cognitive Behavioral Therapy
    (CBT) | SELF-HELP / Personal Growth / General.

Classification: LCC RC489.N47 R58 2018 (print) | LCC RC489.N47
    (ebook) | DDC 616.891/425--dc23.

www.CreatingChangeLifeCoaching.com
Virginia@CreatingChangeLifeCoaching.com

Edited by Nancy Pile: http://www.zoowrite.com

Interior book design and formatting by Angie Mroczka: https://authorgeek.com

Cover design by Ida Sveningsson: http://www. idafiasveningsson.se/?like_it=722

In appreciation for your
purchase of my book, I would like to give you
the Audiobook version 100% FREE
as my way of saying Thank You!

DOWNLOAD AT:
https://creatingchange.readleads.com

Dedication

This book is dedicated to my husband, my dearest friend.

We have shared forty-three years of life together,
two wonderful children and their spouses, and three
engaging grandchildren. Without my husband's love,
encouragement, unending support, honesty, and self-
sacrifice, my life, as it is today, would not have been
achievable. This book also would not have come to fruition.
Stanley, you have, once again, encouraged my voice.
Thank you.

*This book is in honor of people everywhere who
struggle to deal with life's circumstances comfortably.*

Acknowledgments

Without the education and hands-on support of the Self-Publishing School (SPS), this book would have stayed a glimmer in my eye. The entire SPS Community is a remarkable on-line community filled with members that contribute to each other and the group daily. It has been a blessing to be a part of that membership for the past several years.

I thank Chandler Bolt for his inspiration and desire to want to share his accumulated knowledge and experience and to build a community of best-selling authors. I thank Sean Sumner for his total commitment to the position of community manager and his phenomenal support to the multitudes of us wannabe writers. His consistently immediate responses, as he watch-dogged our needs, has been a testament to his dedication and caring. www.self-publishingschool.com

I owe extensive thanks to Nancy Pile, who creatively and enthusiastically edited *Reframe Your Viewpoints*. She fine-tuned and strengthened the manuscript to meet my expectations and help deliver a comprehensive product to those struggling to find peace. I am grateful for the professionalism and experience she brought to my book project. www.zoowrite.com

Angie Mroczka has been invaluable to me in navigating the stressfulness of the electronic world and the Internet requirements to launch this book effort. I am truly thankful for her coaching, patience, understanding, and guidance through it all. Her formatting expertise and her personally constructed Internet tools in addition to her knowledge has been a goldmine to this effort. www.authorgeek.com

I am thankful I took the challenge and chose to share my journey in the form of a book, but it would not have culminated in the publication of *Reframe Your Viewpoints* without the SPS community's support and the friendships I have been privileged to share. These friends will always hold a special place within my heart, and I thank each and every one of the many SPS friends I have been so blessed to have journeyed with.

Finally, I am thankful to Dr. Joe Brown for his support of the content in this book and to the friends and family members who have taken the time to read and comment on earlier drafts of this book. Their efforts were invaluable to me.

If writing a book has ever been a glimmer in your eye, the information available and the community of support through Self-Publishing School is invaluable. At the end of this book, you will find a link to the Self-Publishing School information. I encourage you to explore the idea of becoming an author.

Contents

Chapter 1

Why This Book?
Welcome to Hope, Balance, and Confidence

We are like an artist who is frightened by his own drawing of a ghost. Our creations become real to us and even haunt us.

—Thich Nhat Hanh—

Have you been living at the mercy of your thoughts and fearing your own "drawing of a ghost?"

Do you live with frequent or continuous levels of stress? Have the anxiety, stress, and tension that your mind creates become so real to you that you feel haunted and overwhelmed some of the time?

Are you desperately in need of hope, balance, and confidence so that you can—and will—find a way out of your stress, tension, and anxiety?

Reframing Your Viewpoints is here for you.

In *Reframing Your Viewpoints* you will find tools, strategies, examples, and thorough background information so that you can gain control over those run-away worries and experience significant personal growth. With this book, you will learn:

➢ How to bring better balance into your life

➢ How to lessen your doubts

➢ How to bring inner peace to your days

➢ How to bring confidence and balance into your relationships

➢ How to clearly see through your mental chatter

➢ How to make action, rather than passivity, your mode of operation

➢ How to harness your rightful entitlement to function anxiety-free

➢ How to feel more in control

Reframing Your Viewpoints offers a dynamic tool and 8 supportive building-block strategies that can solve your problems with stress and anxiety. By working with this dynamic tool and the 8 strategies, over time, you will develop a reliable resource that you can put into practice when you sense anxiety, stress, or tension trying to take over. With the toolbox of strategies at your disposal, you will be able to stop those uncomfortable feelings and quickly use them to achieve a sense of calm and peace.

Employing this dynamic tool and the 8 building-block strategies will take time, practice, and reflection, but the calm and peace you gain will eventually become automatic, rapid, and far-reaching.

Let me tell you about the dynamic tool *Reframing Your Viewpoints* offers. The tool is called reframing, which, in this context, means selecting the appropriate words that will cause a noticeable shift in your perception of a situation—from one of heightened stress or fear—to one of reduced emotional stress, calm, and freedom.

Reframing Your Viewpoints presents this reframing tool in clear, concise steps and with multiple examples, plus the necessary background information, so you can employ it immediately to experience its complete and profound effect. Reframing is the central tool of this book.

Reframing Your Viewpoints offers 7 different variations of this powerful reframing tool:

> ➢ The "Going to the SPA" Reframing Technique

> ➢ Reframing Through Forgiveness

> ➢ Asking the "What If . . . Question" Reframing Method

> ➢ Back-door Approach Reframing

> ➢ Understanding Both Perspectives Reframing

> ➢ Reality-check Method of Reframing

> ➢ Giving It to God Reframing—A Variation for Faith-based Readers

With these 7 varieties for reframing, thoroughly presented, explained, exemplified, and in your toolbox, you won't find yourself at a loss and drowned in fear when anxiety starts to strike. By reading, reflecting upon, and practicing reframing, you'll be ready to circumvent that anxiety and achieve the calm, peace, and joy you so desperately seek.

In addition to the dynamic reframing technique, this book presents 8 building-block strategies to learn and incorporate into your reframing practice in order to strengthen the reframing tool so that it becomes even more effective and far-reaching:

> ➢ Strategy 1 Mindfulness

> ➢ Strategy 2 Visual Imagery

> ➢ Strategy 3 Self-awareness

> ➢ Strategy 4 Insightfulness

> ➢ Strategy 5 Forgiveness

> ➢ Strategy 6 Empathy

> ➢ Strategy 7 Habit Formation

> ➢ Strategy 8 Risk-taking

These strategies build upon one another and form a supporting foundation for the technique of reframing. As with reframing, you will find each of these strategies presented in full, including important background information, examples, and recommendations on how to practice them. This will help you master each one as you progress on your journey to take back control of your life.

I like to call this path to taking back control of your life—your "journey of entitlement." What I mean by this is that it is your birthright to be in charge of your life and to clearly make decisions that can lead you to a better place where you do not stay trapped in fear by the picture you have drawn from your thoughts and your perceptions of life.

Reframing and the corresponding building-block strategies will provide you with the armament to claim that birthright. It's up to you to take the necessary steps! There is so much waiting for you on the other side of fear.

> *Growth is painful. Change is painful. But nothing is as painful as staying stuck somewhere you do not belong.*
>
> —Amanda Hale—

Overview

REFRAMING is a strategically powerful tool. It is my dream that every person learn how to decrease their levels of anxiety and turn problems into opportunities by starting to use the reframing technique today.

EVERYBODY experiences stress and anxiety to varying degrees. Stress is a universal problem. I want to demonstrate the remarkable power of reframing to release your stress energy, transform it into productive energy, and change your doubts into fruitful action. When you discover and affirm the power of the reframing tool, I ask that you help bring the term REFRAMING into general public awareness through word of mouth.

Generally speaking, reframing is a term used mostly within the clinical world of counseling. The general population has never heard of it. If everybody was familiar with the technique and the benefit of reframing, it could have significant impact on everyone's life. When reframing becomes a household term, more people will recognize they have an option and a method with which to effectively handle their internal stresses more successfully. Our population, in general, needs to learn about reframing.

It is my desire to partner with you in your quest to bring peace into your life. Partnership with the reader means recognizing each reader has a different learning style or appreciation of subject matter. Therefore, I invite you to assemble the chapter sequence to match your needs. I had a definite purpose to the chapter sequence I laid out, but I understand that that sequence may not be a fit for everyone buying this book.

My desire to help people is greater than my need to teach or coach; therefore, I respect your needs and I offer you the flexibility to steer yourself to your new freedom if you feel you need to re-arrange the flow. It is my hope you will give yourself the greatest likelihood of success by revisiting any skipped sections at some point in order to understand the holistic approach I have assembled. You will not find as comprehensive a plan elsewhere.

I am providing you with one-stop shopping. Each component of this plan is readily available information with today's Internet access but each component is discussed in isolation as an individual technique rather than as a collective process for calming. I am saving you time because I have assembled them in one place so that they can be connected and support each other.

Reframe Your Viewpoints is a holistic blueprint for change. The various chapter contents were strategically included to address all the components of how to make changes in your life. My coaching niches are personal coaching for creating changes in life and relationship coaching. The purpose of this book is to share the pathway to resolving unrest in all aspects of your life through building your relationship with yourself. I sincerely recommend taking the time to read all the information because each chapter provides an understanding to the individual components of transformation.

I was no better equipped to transform my life than you—I have become what I am because of this pathway. Reading less than the entire book would be like telling you there is a buried treasure waiting for you but not providing you with the detailed map.

Reading and understanding the background information on tension, stress, and anxiety, and their physiological effects on your body, which you'll encounter in chapter 3, will give you valuable health rationale so that you can feel you are making informed decisions toward achieving your goals that can give you the profound and lasting peace you so desire.

Adding to the health rationale provided in chapter 3, chapter 4 presents the concepts of two theories—Choice Theory which introduces the premise that our behaviors are subconscious choices and the theory of Multiplicity—that provides an explanation of how your internal "personalities," so to speak, are configured.

As the concepts behind both theories are integral to understanding and employing reframing, the information provided in chapter 4 provides an indispensable foundation for the rest of the book. Understanding multiplicity, just like learning about the reframing tool is information the general population would benefit from learning about.

If textbook information holds little interest for you, feel free to jump ahead to chapter 5. You can always refer back to the foundational chapters after capturing the strategies and techniques for this holistic plan.

Chapters 5 to 9 describe the 8 strategies that augment your understanding and deepen the effectiveness and quality of the reframing tool in your life. For each strategy, you'll find a thorough, step-by-step explanation, background information to answer any "why" questions you may have, examples of the strategy being employed, and suggested ways for you to practice each strategy.

Chapter 10 presents the reframing tool. Chapter 11 discusses our developmental worlds and reviews and ties together the components of this comprehensive blueprint for change. Chapter 12 talks about the time frame needed to bring change into your life.

Combining all of the elements you learn about in *Reframing Your Viewpoints* will lead to lasting changes in how you experience life. Combine your practice of reframing with the 8 building-block strategies and over time, your entire perspective on life will be affected.

What Qualifies Me? — My Background

I love people and gain great satisfaction from helping others, which is why I became a certified life coach. Nothing is more exciting or rewarding to me than helping others discover their potential, helping them meet their inner needs and desires, and partnering with them to create and bring to fruition the changes their hearts are seeking.

Life coaching has allowed me to witness many occasions when a person's eyes pop open in surprise as they unveil a deep yearning that causes them to make a resolution and set a new goal, hear an inner voice they had not heard before, gain a new understanding about some aspect of a situation, or learn something meaningful about themselves.

I have seen many people move through their concerns to attain clarity in their thinking through the use of reframing. I know this process works, researchers know this process works and I see it work regularly in situations every day. There is so much waiting for you beyond your mental chatter.

Prior to becoming a life coach, I have worked for 25 years as a registered dental hygienist (I still practice dental hygiene on a part-time basis). As a dental hygienist, I have helped patients develop the *desire* and skills to perform good oral hygiene, including flossing (not most people's desire).

Because I partner with my patients to understand their time constraints, learn what their motivating factors are, educate them, and support their needs, hundreds of people now make informed dental choices to modify and establish lasting good oral hygiene habits.

After working in dental hygiene for about 12 years while simultaneously navigating my own depression (I will detail that further in the next chapter), I felt a need to understand how the mind works and decided to further my education by returning to school to complete a BS with a concentration in psychology.

Following the undergraduate degree and having a continuing desire to learn more in psychology, as well as having gained so much benefit from my own years of receiving clinical psychological counseling, I enrolled in a master in clinical social work (MSW) program to become a clinical social worker.

More than halfway through the coursework and internships associated with the MSW program, I realized that the field of social work was going to frustrate me with so many required bureaucratic restrictions and paperwork that provide limited paths to resolution for clients. I decided to seek another pathway on which to meet my goal of helping others and cheered when I chose to embark on the creative path of life coaching.

Life coaching allows me to help others discover solutions to situations that have been eating away at them for days, months, or even years, especially in family relationships. As much as we love and need our families, they are probably the source of our most emotionally challenging interpersonal relationships.

I know *Reframing Your Viewpoints* will help you to navigate important relationships in your life, whether it is those complex family relationships or others. Those relationships are challenging because we care so much about the people in our families. We share a history of love, memories, hurts, disappointments, and unresolved feelings between one another. Relationships with our employers and co-workers run neck-to-neck for second place in creating our internal stresses.

The first step in motivating people is to help them see and understand their need for change. Providing examples of reframing, demonstrating the measureable reduction in stress levels, and talking about my own experience will edify the benefits of reframing and expose you to this opportunity and path for potential change. I spend a fair amount of time offering personal examples to serve as illustrations to augment, reinforce and clarify the text allowing you a visual understanding and to bring the text to life.

Feeling a desire to set new goals, committing to initiating the establishment of new habits, and making informed choices enable forward movement. These are the objectives I hope writing this learning guide will help you to accomplish. This guide is filled with interconnected information and human-interest examples to provide readers with basic skills and interwoven concepts, theories, and strategies to help promote an understanding of the whys and hows of human dynamics.

Before we get started with the foundational and building-block information needed to learn reframing and embark on this journey, I need to share a piece of my story, so you can understand how I came to use and depend on reframing, and how it has impacted me. Sharing the value of reframing in my life is WHY I wrote this book.

My Why's

It was about 20 years ago that I began my journey from feeling helpless and being in a clinically depressed state to achieving a more peaceful, calm life where I was not always thinking about how the other person was judging me. I want you to benefit—and much more quickly—from all that I've learned over the past 20 years.

I want you to understand the new, better life that I've managed to achieve from my experiences, reading, and practice of reframing so you can believe it is something within your reach.

At age 46 and into our twenty-third year of marriage, our son returned to his third year of college, my husband left for one of his three-month long business trips to South Korea, and our daughter left home to attend boarding school for the first time all within a one-month period.

I was totally alone and felt abandoned; however, I could not understand that *abandonment* was what I was feeling and certainly could not have put those feelings into words! The loneliness and sadness were overwhelming. Getting out of bed everyday to go to work became my most difficult task of the day. I was unable to understand what was happening to me.

I tried to distract myself with repair and painting projects around the house because I had always enjoyed delving into those activities, but I could not summon the energy, interest, or stamina to stay focused on those tasks. I would end up in a heap on the floor in tears. That is when I realized that I was seriously depressed and that I needed professional help.

Through clinical therapy, I began to understand that I had been living with generalized tension and stress all my life. I also felt that I did not seem to know who I was—I felt I was living behind a mask of calm and that I was detached from my emotions.

I could not easily discern my needs and feelings, and I found it very stressful to verbalize anything I needed to say. I had always focused all my mental energy on satisfying everybody else's needs, which distracted me from connecting to my own heart, needs, and desires.

Over a period of about ten years, I went through cognitive behavioral therapy, forms of talk therapy (individual and group), some PTSD (post traumatic stress disorder) treatment with EMDR (eye-movement desensitization reprocessing), all in conjunction with years of my own bibliotherapy (reading book after book).

All of the counseling, books, and post-therapy higher education goals were profoundly helpful in my gaining insight.

I arrived at a point in therapy where I understood my past: how it had shaped me and how and why I had created the survival techniques I had. I understood that I had invented all my rules to live by so that I could not possibly be unacceptable to others and, therefore, would not be abandoned (a fear derived from a hospitalization experience I will discuss in chapter 3).

I subconsciously rationalized that if I was not a burden to others and if I did not expose anything about myself to others' judgments or let them really know who I was or what parts of me I found shameful, then I would be acceptable to them. I subconsciously rationalized that if I lived by those rules, I would be safe from rejection and abandonment. In my mind's eye, I had decided that in order to survive I needed to obey all my rules. It was a PLAN!

As a child, I had learned to cut myself off from my feelings and needs so that I marched on in life without really existing or experiencing life as it should be experienced. I was disengaged from life. I was numb and suffered from anhedonia, the inability to feel pleasure or joy. These are all classic symptoms of PTSD.

My set of rules, so I thought, made it almost impossible for anyone to abandon or dislike me. I believed my set of rules would keep me safe. My set of rules also made me invisible to others—I was a nondescript entity that filled space, and I made no creative contribution to life other than to live by the rules I had created, which were not beneficial to anyone, least of all me.

Talk about angst and doubt—I had no room for anything else because I was always on my toes anticipating everyone else's needs and striving to please everyone around me. This produced significant inner stress.

Most importantly, I was short-changing my family by not providing the full depth of what I could be, not sharing my opinions and experiences or fully embracing their love for me.

My set of rules also cut off my connection to my heart, feelings, pain, and the knowledge of who I was. I did not know myself. I had created the "ghost," like the one referred to in Thich Nhat Hanh's quote at the beginning of this chapter. It is for those of you who are living that existence, to some varying degree, that I am writing this book.

As we all know, pleasing everyone is an impossible job at best! I know that the rules I set up for myself are similar to the rules that so many people have constructed for themselves in order to keep themselves safe and free from conflict. People need to know this occurs in each of us to varying degrees and that they are not alone. That is also WHY I wrote this book.

I now appreciate what I have accomplished. I am finally able to give my opinions and life experiences value and believe those will have value to others: this too is WHY I am writing this book. I want to use my VOICE to help other people. Let me add too that my family has noted the positive improvements, and they embrace the benefits daily.

I share all this, so you can see where I started and how far I've come. Your understanding of my personal story not only establishes my credentials with you—from it I want you to gain inspiration, hope, and excitement for the incredible transformation you are about to undergo as you start your journey.

I believe my personal story complements the information presented throughout as illustrations of actual real-life scenarios to demonstrate how the context offered in this learning guide is to be understood.

Let me share the knowledge I have researched and collected over my twenty-year journey. Let me save you from that overwhelmingly time-consuming task so that the likelihood of your success at finding peace in your life may be achieved more quickly and is more probable.

I hope this book inspires you enough to read it more than once and to also return to sections of it as a reference guide. The information will be further assimilated with every reading of the different sections.

In order to create changes in your life, you will need to develop a **mindset**. With a patient, understanding, avidly determined mindset that places your baby-step goals as your highest daily priority, change will occur. Make your daily goals tiny strides to keep them from being overwhelming, yet when added together provide you with daily proof of progress.

> *There are two types of pain in this world: Pain that hurts you and pain that changes you.*
>
> —Unknown—

A Glimpse at Reframing

Below are a couple of brief examples of reframing in order to give you a taste of where this book—and you—are headed. Further along in the book, I will unpack the reframing process into steps so that you have complete information for practicing this powerful technique yourself.

For now, it will be fun and beneficial for you to get a quick glimpse of where you are headed.

SAMPLE REFRAMING 1

Your mother-in-law is coming to visit tomorrow, and when she walks in, she always makes a comment about how small your house is.

Just contemplating her arrival and this comment puts you on edge. You feel the tension invading your shoulders and brow. Your pulse quickens.

Aware of this anxiety and tension coming upon you, you decide to reframe your viewpoint. You stop, take a deep breath to initiate a sense of calm and call on yourself to create an alternate scenario—an **alternate thought**—of how you would like her arrival to play out. To form your **alternate thought**, start to calm yourself and assume control by taking one or two deep breaths to center and focus your thoughts.

Alternate thought: our home is our castle! We are exceedingly happy in our life together, our community, and our home. I will make that statement to my mother-in-law when she speaks this time. I will not allow her to diminish my family, my life, or me.

You finish with another deep breath.

By creating a positive neutral statement, you actively reframe your perspective of dreading her arrival to one of taking back your control, which allows you to eagerly anticipate her arrival so you can deliver your statement and end this reoccurring anxiety.

You can now sense the tension, stress, and anxiety decreasing in your shoulders, brow, and mind. You feel entitled to take back control of the situation from her judgmental comments. The tension is easing *because* you have decided to take action.

SAMPLE REFRAMING 2

You are in a hurry driving to work because you are a little late getting out the door. You encounter a school bus stopping to pick up children, and you are forced to stop your car when you see the red stop sign swing out from the side of the bus.

There are a large number of children, and it takes several minutes for them to load onto the bus and get fully seated before the driver can close the door and get moving. You are finding it difficult to hang onto your patience while you see mothers giving hugs and saying goodbye to their kids or teenagers joking around with each other, all of which increases the amount of time you have to sit and wait.

Meanwhile, you anticipate arriving even later to work—you have a very busy day ahead. You can feel the tension in your jaw, arms, and shoulders, alerting you to your increasing stress level. You recognize what is taking place within you, so you immediately choose to employ reframing. You initiate a cleansing breath, bringing back your focus and control, and then you seek an **alternate thought**.

Alternate thought: being a little late to work is really not such a big deal. I will handle my schedule. I do not arrive habitually late. My co-workers and boss will hardly notice, and they know I am a diligent worker.

You might create a second **alternate thought**: I am thankful we have a law in place to protect these children and transport them safely to and from school. An injury to any of these children could potentially devastate so many lives connected to the injured child. This law is an important law and is based on previous incidences where those restrictions were not in place and families suffered needless tragedy.

You take a deep breath and sense the level of calm that has returned to your mind and muscles. What is important for you to start to grasp, is the self-awareness skill you will need to develop in order to detect the *presence* of tension in your body as quickly as it arises so that you can insert the reframing technique that will restore calm. The speed at which you become aware of your tension will be at the core of your success for inserting the reframing technique.

THREE QUICKIE REFRAMES

Here are two questions you can ask yourself when you find yourself in the midst of mental chaos to help you alter your perspective as well as three simple statements that offer you a moment to step back and assess reality. They have the potential to halt your doubts and chatter very quickly and perpetuate a reframing moment:

1. What advice would you give to your best friend in this situation on how to handle it? Then listen to your own advice.

2. If you had a friend going through a similar time where they felt guilt, shame or criticism towards themself, would you judge them or feel empathy for that friend? Could you not allow that same empathy toward them to be extended to you?

3. Three Statements: It is what it is; I am who I am; I am where I am supposed to be at this time and will be here until I am ready for the next step.

Chapter Wrap-up

Reframing Your Viewpoints offers a dynamic tool—reframing—that, in conjunction with the 8 supportive building-block strategies, will allow you to free yourself from anxiety and stress to experience life from a new perspective—one of hope, joy, and peace.

Starting from a place of anxiety, depression, and discomfort in life, I have spent 20 years refining and enhancing, the reframing technique to incorporate the 8 additional building-block strategies. By incorporating the 8 strategies, I believe I offer you a holistically calming plan. My goal is for you to benefit from all that I have learned and practiced so that you can attain comfort in life more quickly than I.

The reframing technique can and should be used starting today. However, the process of incorporating the 8 building-block strategies into your reframing practice, yielding a comprehensive plan to attack stress and anxiety in your life will develop more gradually. This comprehensive plan is not going to fall into place today. It will be like any process—a gradual pathway.

This comprehensive plan will require learning, practice, baby-step progress, patience and the belief and trust that your diligent consistent efforts will culminate in a life stabilized by clarity of thought and a peaceful mental state. I am suggesting you stretch the limits of your mind as you enter this galaxy of self-led exploration and believe in the freedom that can evolve from that.

Reframing Your Viewpoints offers you an opportunity to begin a life-enriching journey starting today that will lead to a fresh perspective and hope for your worldview. I invite you to give yourself the gift of living a hopeful, joyful life by reading this book. It is time to lead yourself to a better place. There are all types of prisons in this world—could this be your key to freedom?

Change is a process, not an event.

—Unknown—

Your Action Plan

Prepare to ignite your inner potential as you embark on this life-changing endeavor. Engage in this exploration and adventure with an open heart and open mind—and make it fun! However you pace yourself and in whatever style you move through this book, I encourage you to read the entire book because without the full spectrum of what I present and discuss, you may not understand how it all ties together into this comprehensive plan.

Reframing Your Viewpoints presents material that will require a level of study and dedication on your part. You have the freedom to grow with this book in a style most comfortable for you. Being comfortable means giving yourself the time to enjoy the journey.

You need time to reflect upon, assimilate, and process insights before moving on to new material. Give yourself time between each chapter for practice, exercises, experiments, and thorough reflection on the material presented. Respect yourself and your needs by moving at your own pace. Do not let life rush you and do not criticize yourself.

Chapter 2 explains the malleable capacity of the human brain that allows all of us to potentially alter how we interface with our lives.

What is Waiting for You?
What You Can Expect?

Whether you think you can or you think you can't—you're right.

—Henry Ford—

In chapter 2 you will be compiling background knowledge about how the brain works, so you can better understand how dedicated practice of the reframing technique, as well as the other 8 strategies given in this book, offers you a new way of restructuring your brain's functionality so that you can permanently take back control of your life.

Neuroplasticity, Reframing, and You

There comes a point where you need to take the next step—start living a new kind of life.

Reality-based functioning in life requires you to remove or lower your self-created barriers, address thought patterns from your earlier years, and live as a fully engaged adult to the greatest extent possible.

As I moved away from regular counseling in order to reengage in life with a clearer understanding and knowledge of the opportunities before me, I clung to the reframing technique that I was taught in my initial exposure to clinical therapy—cognitive behavioral therapy.

It worked very well, and reframing became my lifeline. I began to use it again and again. Not only when I became aware of my mental chatter, but also when I needed to reframe my understanding of other people, and when I wanted to take on challenges, overcome obstacles, and insert some risk-taking. I used the reframing method again and again because it worked.

It is common knowledge that our brains have a high degree of neuroplasticity. Plasticity means adaptability, so the brain's neuroplasticity refers to the surprising ease at which the brain's neurons can be adapted or "rewired," so to speak.

In essence, scientists have discovered that a person's brain isn't set. It's not rigid. Instead, groups of brain cells that once performed only one function can gradually adapt to perform additional tasks or function in a different way. And this is a good thing. It offers each of us many possibilities for growth, change and hope.

The knowledge and understanding of the adaptability of brain cells has only been researched and demonstrated within this past century. Psychiatric researcher and psychoanalyst Norman Doidge, MD, has written many books on the subject of creating change in the brain. In *The Brain That Changes Itself*, Doidge states, "Thinking can turn on parts of our brains . . . we can rewire our brains with our thoughts."

His book provides case studies on stroke victims, people struggling with learning disorders, people with obsessive compulsiveness, and trauma victims who changed their thinking and behavior through thought and activity. With this type of therapy, people are able to resume function in life despite having been affected by stroke, etc.

Turning on new areas of the brain through thinking or acting in new ways creates new connections to that stroke-damaged area. This allows new functional support from a different area of the brain where the cells have not been damaged by stroke. Essentially, because of the brain's neuroplasticity, they could "rewire" their weakened areas of brain function to restore healthy adaptive brain functionality.

The brain's neuroplasticity also comprises the potential for the formation of new neural connections that can be established that reroute old thinking paths to create new thinking paths for the interpretation of incoming stimulus.

This neuroplasticity can occur on a neurological cellular level or with cortical remapping. Meaning, every part of the body is connected to a specific site in the brain (creating a map of pathways) and is dependent upon that site for its sensory input and motor control.

In cortical remapping, if a person suffers an amputation, the pathway between the amputation site and it's corresponding site in the brain no longer exists. That part of the brain that was in charge of the amputated limb will be taken over by adjacent cortical regions (areas in the brain).

This new neural pathway establishes connection to another part of the body. In other words, the brain cells, which previously communicated with the amputated limb, will gradually form a new connection and sensory route to a different part of the body.

The beginning of neuroplastic changes in your mind can begin as soon as consistent use of the reframing technique and the 8 strategies is initiated.

Collectively employing this cohesive plan has created cognitive changes in my thinking because of the new neural pathways formed in my brain. My consistently more beneficial reaction-to-life responses (lower stress, clarity in resolution, and confidence) demonstrate the permanent adaptation of how I function in life.

Reframing helped me to redefine my entire outlook and attitude on life. Now, I rarely need to purposefully reframe because, due to all the active reframing I've practiced over the years, new neural pathways have been created that alter the way in which I *process* the incoming information such that it does not create inner anxiety.

The new experiences collected over the years through continuous risk-taking and reframing practice have provided me with a new reservoir of memories based upon reality that are stored in the brain's hippocampus.

Having lived with generalized anxiety from very early in life, my memories have all been configured from a fearful or emotional perspective and those memories in my brain were stored in the amygdala (a' · mig · da · la). Previously, the memories stored in the amygdala controlled all my behaviors, which is why I reacted to life from out of a fear perspective.

With every situation in life we encounter, the human mind automatically goes through a process of interpretation to figure out how we should respond. This occurs within nanoseconds. If our reactions have always been configured from a fearful reference point, we will not have a balanced view of life from which to operate and make decisions.

With the establishment of new neural pathways, when a potentially fearful situation is encountered, the information routes to the hippocampus (hip·pa'·cam·pus) to retrieve a positive memory experience rather than the amygdala to retrieve a fearful memory. This is a change in how I process information. This re-routing occurs through NLP (neuro-linguistic programming) and the reframing technique is based upon NLP.

The use of alternative words (linguistics) based on reality produces improved behavior. Improved behavior creates a positive memory. The positive memory elicits confidence in decision-making. Gradually, the collection of positive memories forms a new reference point from which to interpret a situation, and that leads to consistent behavior changes.

The following diagram outlines the incoming path of the stimulus prior to NLP—going through the amygdala (old reference point) where fearful memories are stored and anxiety results. Historically, perhaps this has been your mental traffic pattern.

Following the usage of NLP, the diagram shows the incoming stimulus traveling through the hippocampus (new reference point) where reference points based on reality are stored and confidence results.

These are the neurological changes that reframing and the 8 strategies will contribute to. Building new reality-based memories will make the hippocampus your new reference resource.

This is a lot of information to follow, which is why I recommend keeping this book on your bookshelf as a resource to refer back to after you have finished reading it. Information is the key to understanding and understanding is the catalyst to personal growth.

When we learn the why's, the how come's, and the what for's, we can slowly piece together a vision for why there is a need to change. Through understanding, the benefits poised on our horizons become desires and our desires develop into our goals. Goals lead to self-growth.

STRESSFUL SITUATION

After reframing, the mind interprets the situation from a collection of recent memories (stored in the hippocampus) that are based on reality. Consequently, logic is available to handle the situation without panic or indecision.

If a challenging situation had followed the old route to the amygdala where old fearful memories are stored, reactions would continue to be based on fearful misperceptions. Because responses to situations now stem from experiences based on reality, stress or anxiety is rarely elicited because there is a much more realistic core understanding of day-to-day situations, peoples' motives, and one's value to others.

These realistic understandings reflect the establishment of the new lasting neural pathways that the deliberate practice of reframing over the years will help to create in your brain. These neurological changes to the brain are reflected in consistently clearer thinking, improved choices or behavior, and a lack of generalized and social anxiety. That is my hope for you.

The reframing techniques will train the mind to view life from a healthy perspective. The self-doubts and voices will be quieted and gradually replaced with optimism and energy to take risks and experiment in life without fear.

The fear will have been replaced with confidence, a sense of adventure, and excitement because the experimental risk-taking proves anxiety-ridden perceptions are not based on reality.

During a fearful moment, it is very difficult to separate reality from our apprehensions prior to the establishment of the new neural pathways that will be constructed through reframing and risk-taking. Reframing will help you understand that reality, in general, is non-threatening.

Do I ever have moments of fear and doubt? Yes, but only fleetingly and such moments are not sustained because I become immediately aware of the intrapersonal dynamics working in my mind and cognitively choose to **STOP** the cycle, harness the fear, embrace it, and purposefully change my thinking perspective by reframing.

Continuous self-awareness of the perspectives and attitudes playing in your mind can alert you to an awareness of the need to make a new choice. Instead of remaining in a stressful state, you can choose to create a change in your thinking or perspective by using the reframing tool.

I am living an entirely different life because of reframing, I am now sensitized to quickly and clearly detect (become aware) when the negative voices in my mind begin to sabotage my behaviors and choices. When I detect them, I choose to take my mind to a healthier place. I choose to harness my stress. This is self-awareness and this is why developing self-awareness is critical to enabling personal growth.

It may turn out for some of you that some amount of face-to-face counseling or a particular method of therapy might be helpful or necessary. You may find that you are not gaining the insights very quickly to help you get to know yourself. If that becomes the case, what you learn from this book will help to quicken any therapy process because you will have a slight jump on understanding some basic principles.

Counseling or behavioral therapy is not something to be afraid of. It certainly might scare you to think of exposing your inner thoughts to someone as intimately as counseling requires. However, it can be an essential component for your path to a more enjoyable life.

Counselors have pretty much heard everything, they have worked through layers of their own issues, they are people helpers—nothing surprises them. As a group, they are non-judgmental and very safe people to talk to. I encourage you to take that step if you feel stuck. It will help to set you free.

> *When you know yourself, you are EMPOWERED. When you accept yourself, you are INVINCIBLE.*
>
> —Tina Lifford—

Reframing's Essential Components

Learning to reframe life will require being your own best friend, intimacy with yourself, and practice—a lot of practice. Being your own best friend means listening and giving value to yourself, not judging yourself, and accepting all aspects of yourself.

Learning to reframe life will not require any monetary output (other than the purchase of this book), no special space to perform and practice your skills, and no special clothing, equipment, or expensive lessons. Learning to reframe your life will require persistence but not huge chunks of time out of your day.

Fitting the building-block skills and reframing into your days can occur within seconds repeated throughout the day. It all takes place inside your head, so only you will know that you are practicing.

Reframing life situations to calm tension, stress, and anxiety in no way means you are denying or minimizing your feelings. On the contrary, knowing how to reframe provides you with the ability to do something about it. Reframing will attend to your feelings by having you acknowledge those feelings, examine them, and take a different path.

Wanting to reframe your life fosters time for you to notice and pay attention to your feelings. Those feelings are seeking your attention as demonstrated by the body's muscle tension, stress symptoms, or anxious mental chatter filling your head and attempting to capture your focus.

The problem with mental chatter is that it is negative energy. We criticize ourselves when we feel confused or stressed, we wish we could get rid of it, and that results in more mental chatter that contributes to and creates more confusion. With reframing, you can harness your attention and energy to focus on the reframing skill that will turn that negative energy into a positive outcome. Mental chatter is cognitive dissonance that *can* be managed.

Reframing, as defined in the textbook, *Contemporary Behavior Therapy,* fits into the "cognitive restructuring" framework of cognitive-behavioral therapy. Cognitive restructuring involves recognizing maladaptive thinking processes (momentary dysfunctionality) and substituting those for more workable cognitions.

Cognitive restructuring therapy maintains that people construct their realities based on what is important, meaningful, and real to them. In other words, the interpretations you *assign* to an event, rather than the actual event itself, determines its effect on your emotions.

Reframing will allow you to reconstruct your thoughts in order to view circumstances from a new perspective, thus leading you to feel more positive about that same circumstance and, therefore, to feel less fear or stress.

This learning guide is intended to start an awareness process in you that will lead to a deeper understanding of who you are, why you feel certain ways, and how your thinking affects your behavior. Tony Robbins calls it "Heart Intelligence" because he maintains that brain waves are connected to heart waves. Robbins recommends you "breathe through your heart" in order to identify where you need to take yourself. Become curious about you!

My goal is to ignite movement within you so that you will lead yourself in finding peace and creating healthy relationships both within yourself and with those important people in your life. In order to bring change into your life, you need to develop some new skills and turn those skills into habits.

Practice of the building-block strategies will be valuable in helping to create the reframing habit. You have access at http://bit.ly/ReframeExercise to download the complimentary Reframing Exercises and Supplemental Information Packet. I have also constructed a fillable SPA Exercise Template you can download here http://bit.ly/ReframeSPA.

This book not only teaches the reframing technique and presents the 8 strategies, it links them together to create a cohesive plan for you to implement into your reframing practice. This book applies that plan to real-life situations, case studies, and hypothetical situations that stem from my 20-year personal journey as well as from my professional experience as a life coach and dental hygienist.

Reframing your life can become automatic over time. The more regularly you practice it, the more it will be the habit of choice and the go-to technique you employ. Reframing will become ingrained as your first method of dealing with life's stresses. Eventually, you can reach the point of living almost free of doubt. During those times when you still experience some residual doubt, you can return to reframing and trust it to safely take you to a peaceful place.

You will never change your life
until you change something
you do daily.

—John C. Maxwell—

Be sure to allow yourself as much time as it may take. You can break the plan into steps, taking one strategy at a time and getting comfortable with that one before moving onto the next strategy.

However, far you travel in this journey and to whatever varying degree you ultimately use reframing, I am confident that you will reduce the level of stress in your life to a better and healthier level. Simply cultivating your awareness of the stress and that you have options will put control back into your hands.

SAMPLE STRESSFUL SITUATION

Imagine you have been working like crazy at a project needed for work. You have logged in hours and hours of effort without taking a restful break. You have not only been at it during long business hours at the off ce but also at home during your personal time. This has been going on for days.

You are exhausted and can't keep your eyes open to work any longer. Your eyes are burning, and your head is literally nodding off to sleep at your laptop. Your head is so loaded with information, you can't think clearly. You are working at home and decide to take a much-needed break to lie down on the sofa and take a power nap.

BUT sleep does not come. Your mind is filled with negative voices arguing with each other. You can hear scolding, concern, begging, promises, and everything but the needed peace and calm from which to find some rest.

The fun and viewpoint-changing part of reframing comes when you take the self-awareness of all those voices, hear what is taking place in your head, say **STOP** to those voices, and, in this case, choose to go to the so-called SPA.

The "SPA" variation of the reframing technique comes from an acronym crafted by Dr. Joe Brown. There were many years between the termination of my work with Dr. Brown (www.drjosephbrown.com) and beginning my regular use of the SPA technique. However, during that time when I did intermittently use the reframing method, it was tremendously helpful.

Consequently, because there was a span of time between ending therapy with Dr. Brown and consistent use of the SPA technique, I have inadvertently altered his exact letter representation and his technique. It was when I completed all my modes of therapy and needed to be self-reliant, that I constructed what I remembered of his SPA variation for regular use and reframing started to pave my way in life.

Dr. Brown's "SPA" acronym—See your thoughts, Pair them with your feelings and generate alternative thoughts" as well as the precise reframing technique he teaches to his clients has been modified by me to fit what I remembered and to allow for situational variations. I expect you will also modify your reframing to best suit your needs.

EXAMPLE OF THE SPA REFRAMING TECHNIQUE

By chapter 10, you will have gained the background information as well as practice in the foundational building-block strategies, so you'll be ready to learn about reframing in more detail, as well as all of the reframing variations, to begin practicing it completely.

Here, you'll encounter a condensed explanation of the SPA reframing technique—so you can anticipate where we are going and experience a demonstration of the strength of the reframing tool that you will be mastering in the coming weeks.

Using the above scenario about being overtired from work, imagine your fatigue and mental burnout. Hear how your mental chatter is passing judgment on you. You just want to get some sleep! Imagine the anger you are feeling at yourself while you are tossing and turning when trying to get some rest. You are beginning to feel hopelessly caught in a catch-22 loop.

Let's Go to the SPA using my modification of Dr. Brown's Acronym

S—See the anxiety

P—Pheel the feeling

A—Alternate thought to be substituted

START with 1-2 deep cleansing breaths to begin to collect your focus. (This is so important.)

See what you are seeing and hearing: visualize the critical voices scolding you for not having more endurance, for working too slowly, and for not even being able to take advantage of needed nap time. **See** your turmoil in the tossing and turning. These voices heighten your anxiety and keep you in the state of unrest that is preventing you from getting the sleep you so desperately need and want.

Pheel the emotions of shame, embarrassment, anger, or upset that you feel from the perception of thinking you are being weak and indulging yourself by taking time to rest when there is still so much to do and deadlines are looming. **Pheel** the mental struggle you are wrestling with—you are not being efficient because you are so tired, but it is because you are so tired that you can't be efficient.

At this point, assess your level of anxiety on a scale from 1 to 10 (10 being the strongest). By assigning your stress an intensity level (a number) at this point during the SPA treatment, you establish a reference point you can use for comparison to measure your level of reduced stress after you complete the reframing process (your trip to the SPA).

Assess your anxiety level: 7

Alternate thought: let's recognize that the voices are telling you that you do not have the time to take a nap because you will miss your deadline. Now consider this question, "Are those voices trying to *protect* you from a disaster?" Yes! So, if those voices are trying to protect you, can you find a word to describe what role in your life those voices represent? Would those voices represent your support team? Who in your life provides you with support? It's your FRIENDS.

Now, recognize that those critical voices are attempting to act as the voices of FRIENDS. Because the critical voices are jumping into your head to keep you working in order to protect you from failure, they are trying to act like accountability buddies. They are attempting to do what FRIENDS do.

Friends protect friends! There was a time in your past when you needed to stay focused and not get distracted from an assignment. At that time, those critical voices kept you on task by shaming you to get the job done. At that time in your young life those voices were your real friends because they protected you. They provided the attention to task you needed.

Those voices you hear today are your automatic response to an old situation. Those voices are now showing up again as your friends—or at least they think they are protecting you as friends do. The critical voices have good intentions but in your adult life have a poor way of showing it.

In this way, you reconstruct how the situation appears. The voices of criticism are coming to protect you and keep you to task as they did when you were young and easily distracted. You needed their help when you were young—and now, though the situation may seem the same to them, in fact, their help is hindering you.

What to do—acknowledge them by saying hello, thank them for showing up because they promote your self-awareness; BUT assure them that today you have the situation under control.

Assess your anxiety now: it decreased. Now it is down to a 4. Notice this change from 7 to 4 and acknowledge its significance.

Now, consider those voices to be a part of you that has been with you for a very long time—since your childhood. Understand that those voices have, in the past, kept you on target, giving you determination and keeping you from giving up on a job or on yourself. Thank the voices for serving you so well in the past, but today you are not that child who will get distracted or procrastinate.

So many of us identify the voices of our inner friends as judgmental and critical voices—causing us to think we are deficient—without even knowing we've done so!

Notice that you altered your view of the situation—you've reframed your perspective by identifying the voices as voices that used to be old friends, as voices whose intention is to protect and help you. By simply recognizing those voices are your FRIENDS with good intentions, it reduces your shame, anger, and frustration.

Now, take another deep breath and try to find some substitute words, such as *empathy* and *trust*, to replace the *judgment* and *criticism* you hear.

You have agreed that the voices are (or were) your friends. Adult friends would empathize with you and trust you to take care of yourself. You know you will stay on task, you are an adult in control of a realistic schedule, and you are recognizing that you will produce a much better job and bring it to completion—after you have taken a break.

Promise those voices you will return to the job very shortly and that it is OK to take a break. The job will get done on time and with excellent quality. As Dr. Richard Schwartz (to be introduced in chapter 4) teaches his clients—ask those voices to step aside. Ask them to trust you—you will get back to work after a rest. Allow your FRIENDS (the voices) to embrace you as you drift off on your power nap.

Dr. Schwartz recommends assigning those protective parts of yourself a new job after you have had your sleep, are done with the task, and can think clearly. Promise those voices you will visit them again after this workload has been finished and reassign that part of yourself a more relevant job that will be more practical and in line with your adult needs.

Assess your anxiety level again: it feels further reduced to a 2 or 3.

Hopefully, as a result of this SPA reframing example, you have a better idea of how reframing works and a good idea of what you will be learning to do over the course of this book to manage your stress.

This example should allow you the opportunity to gain some insight as to how your critical voices might have evolved and why. You can now make a resolution for the future to understand why and where those voices came from so that when you hear voices of criticism again in the future, you will say "hello" to them, appreciate their support but redirect their effort to a present-day need.

Your voices are your FRIENDS in every circumstance! Understanding this allows you to trust their intent and reframe their purpose in every situation. This reframing combined with deep relaxed breathing could be applied to all your nocturnal struggles.

Let me also add that with consistent, dedicated practice, you'll be able to employ the reframing technique to achieve measurably reduced anxiety and stress—in a matter of seconds. Notice that I wrote—"with consistent, dedicated practice!" Very little in life occurs haphazardly—each of the incremental steps outlined in every chapter are going to contribute to your fortress of protection.

Chapter Wrap-up

Physicist Erwin Schrödinger once stated, "The essence of life is information." It is my hope the information collected and presented in this book adds to your life's essence, contributing to your success at reframing, which will feed your neuroplastic changes. By practicing reframing consistently, you will establish new neural pathways in your brain that will create automatic, beneficial behavioral changes in your thinking and emotions.

With your overview of the "Going to the SPA" variation of reframing you have an increased understanding of one of the reframing variations that you will be mastering by the book's end. You have a basic understanding of how it works, as well as the significant benefits it imparts.

Throughout the book, I welcome your reactions, comments or questions. Please connect with me at Virginia@ CreatingChangeLifeCoaching.com.

Your Action Plan

Consider having a notebook beside you as you read this learning guide so that you can take notes to refer back to. You need to discover opportunities for practicing the building-block skills. Please download the short book, *It's All About the Windows* to read about how to look for opportunities in your daily life that can promote personal growth: https:// www.CreatingChangeLifeCoaching.com

Chapter 3 will help you to understand the physical toll stress and anxiety take on you and where the origin of your stress lies.

Let's Talk About Anxiety

We are not thinking machines that feel. Rather, we are feeling machines that think.

—Antonio D'Amasio—

In this chapter, I will discuss what anxiety, tension, and stress represent and how they impact our bodies so that you can become more self-aware of when your body sends you signs that stress is beginning to sabotage your emotions from things going on in life.

In turn, that awareness will help to remind you that you have a new tool, reframing, and that you have choices in how to handle your anxiety and stress.

Understanding the emotional and physical toll that living with stress takes on your body and health will lead to your making informed choices.

Understanding the origins of tension or anxiety helps to eliminate fear in general and opens the channels to self-knowledge and self-acceptance—both of which help significantly to lower overall stress.

You can use pharmaceuticals to help relieve symptoms of stress. The pharmaceuticals can be effective; however, they can have side effects and they gradually take a toll on the liver.

When you stop taking the pharmaceuticals, the symptoms will return, whereas investing time and effort in creating personal change, will begin the process for a permanent transformation of your anxiety.

Tension, Stress, and the Physiology of Anxiety

*Anxiety is a thin stream of fear trickling through the mind.
If encouraged, it cuts a channel through which all other thoughts are drained.*

—Arthur Somers Roche—

Anxiety stems from two sources: external and internal stressors. External stressors come at us from things going on in our lives, like pressures at work, school pressures, finances, family pressures, busy schedules, and big events, like a job change, housing move, wedding, or major loss (e.g., divorce or death).

Dr. Shawn Talbott, author of *The Cortisol Connection*, notes that anxiety and stress can also be the products of a hectic life, continuous dieting schemes, or sleeplessness.

Internal stressors come from our misperceptions, unrealistic expectations, negative self-beliefs, and past events in our lives that continue to play out to varying degrees when current circumstances trigger a past emotion. Tony Robbins refers to this as our "Core Story."

Anxiety, as taught to me by Dr. Joe Brown, is the physiological manifestation of some level of fear. He assured me that somewhere in my past, I had experienced some kind of traumatic experience. He stated that the magnitude of our present day physiological symptoms of fear is proportional to the magnitude of our original experience.

Fear manifested as anxiety interferes with our ability to see reality. Fear arouses a need in us to avoid, run away from, and not face situations and decisions. Fear confuses and distracts us from logical, linear thinking and planning. Fear keeps us from being able to set goals or formulate and implement cohesive plans.

If you experience continuous levels of fear, it can dominate you. There may be no room for any other feeling to be appreciated or detected because the fear is all encompassing. Your mind may postpone any other decision-making until later if you are consumed with fear. Confusion dominates your thinking.

Whether the fear is real, imagined, or anticipated, the effect on your mind and body is essentially the same—the mind freezes until the threat has been removed, resolved, or eliminated. In a way, certain body functions also freeze.

Let me explain. Increased pulse, breathing and blood pressure will remain elevated throughout a stressful time. Some individuals experience intestinal or stomach discomfort, bloating, or muscular pain during periods of stress.

These physiological changes in the body caused by anxiety occur when the heart and brain ("Heart Intelligence") sense fear and send the message to the adrenal glands to release cortisol and adrenaline into the bloodstream in order for you to position yourself in a fight, flight, or freeze mindset. When equilibrium has been returned, your body will react physiologically by returning your heart rate and breathing to normal, relaxing the tension in your muscles, and resuming the process of digestion.

Continuous emotional tension in your body tightens your muscles, thereby restricting circulation in your veins, arteries, and the lymphatic vessels throughout your body.

When your circulatory system is slowed due to taut muscles, your heart has to work harder to circulate your blood putting undue stress on your heart and reducing the flow of blood to your body's extremities.

Reduced circulation deprives your muscles and organs of the necessary oxygen, nutrients, and enzymes needed by your life-supporting organs to maintain optimum health and keep them fully functional. Learning to recognize body tension throughout your body allows you to take action to reduce muscle tension.

The Symptoms of Anxiety table below shows the many physiological manifestations of anxiety.

SYMPTOMS OF ANXIETY	
Area of Body	**Symptoms**
Head	Mind races, increased worry, headaches, feeling faint light-headed, feel unreal
Mental	Confusion, trouble with memory, depression, inability to focus, obsessive thinking, compulsiveness, OCD, ADD, ADHD
Speech	Stuttering, Tourette's Syndrome
Face	Blushing
Eyes	Blurred vision, spots in front of eyes, become disoriented
Mouth	Dryness, speaking quickly, difficulty swallowing, TMJ pain
Neck/Shoulders	Tense, stiff muscles, muscular pain
Arms/Legs	Tingling sensations, numbness

Muscles	Muscle tension, Fibromyalgia, Myofascial Pain Syndrome,
Respiratory System	Breathing speeds up, taking deeper breaths, difficulty breathing
Chest/Heart	Tightness, palpitations, pain, heart pounds, races or skips a beat
Lower Abdomen	Stomach churns, irritable bowel syndrome, stomachache, nausea, loss of appetite, increase in acid flex
Digestive System	Digestion slows down or stops, feel sick
Legs	Feel wobbly or jel y-like
Feet/Toes	Tingling sensations, numbness
All Over	Feel hot, sweaty, anxiety attacks, social withdrawal, irritability, decreased sex drive, loss of motivation, weakened immune system, fatigue, restlessness, drug or alcohol use
Sleep	Insomnia, Chronic Fatigue Syndrome, prolonged fatigue states, recurrent dreams
Increased Adrenal Hormone Levels	Food cravings, lots of abdominal fat, insulin resistance, high blood sugar, mood swings, high anxiety, brain fog, irritability, stomach ulcer, low immune function causing frequent colds, infections, high blood pressure, disturbed sleep, premature aging, Muscle loss, bone loss, hair loss, skin conditions such as acne, eczema, increased perspiration

A Curious Disconnection and Its Severe Repercussions

The physiological sensations brought on by the stress hormones can be very strong, but sometimes their intensity does not match the intensity of your current situation, which can be confusing to experience. If trying to connect strong physical reactions or emotions to what is going on in the present situation doesn't seem to fit, you might be inclined to dismiss or avoid the physical reactions or emotions as nothing, thinking, "I am just being silly."

However, they should not be dismissed even though you may not understand them. You can safeguard against cellular destruction in your body from the elevated hormone levels by becoming aware of those changes in your body. The adrenal hormones have been released because fears, past or present, are triggering that release.

Awareness of the physiological signs of stress when they occur, will lead to your recognizing when you are in a moment of opportunity where you can choose to insert the reframing habit.

When a current situation triggers an emotion or fear stemming from a childhood experience or trauma, you probably will not be consciously aware of a memory or emotion being triggered. But your "Heart Intelligence" (Tony Robbins) will signal the adrenal glands to kick into gear and that's why you are being flooded with stress and tension but don't understand why.

Even though as a child a fear may not have been reality-based, that fearful childhood situation instantaneously provokes a *tension* memory in the body's muscle tissue that will be locked into the body's smooth and striated muscle fibers (explained below) for years to come.

This is "muscle memory" and it is a real phenomenon, not just an imagined concept. The muscle memory will be recalled throughout life whenever that same emotion is elicited in the present moment by an experience or feeling similar to the original situation. Your "Heart Intelligence" will trigger the release of your stress hormones, and that occurs within you automatically.

An example of smooth muscle fiber is found in the walls of hollow internal structures, like blood vessels or the lining of the stomach and intestines. Hence, when symptoms of indigestion are your response to stress, it is your muscle memory of your smooth muscle tissue that is responding. Smooth muscle tissue is involuntary and has built-in controls from involuntary nerves and hormones. Ah-ha—there are those hormones again.

Skeletal muscle tissue is striated, is attached to your bones, and allows you to move. Its movement is voluntary, meaning you cognitively cause them to contract and relax.

The wall of the heart is composed of cardiac muscle tissue. Cardiac muscle tissue is striated and involuntary. This means your heart is both nerve- and hormone-controlled—therefore, your heart muscle is affected by both your mental thoughts as well as the hormonal changes taking place during stressful situations.

Athletes, dancers, and musicians rely upon muscle memory. They are so practiced in executing finely honed, graceful, smooth and efficient body movements that the muscles memorize those precisions.

The execution of their skills becomes automatic, eliminating the need for the athlete or performer to have to think about the miniscule muscular execution of their skill. By not having to focus on the details of the execution, they can focus on being smoother, faster, more refined, creative, or musical.

How each of us walks and moves every day is dependent upon muscle memory. But muscle memory can also be stimulated by the release of the adrenal hormones.

When a trauma is experienced, hormones are released and the resulting muscle tension is imprinted on the muscles during the moments of the original trauma and will be elicited and replicated in the body's muscles when activated in the future by a similar situation.

An example of a simple childhood trauma might be a mother and young child going around a department store where all the clothing racks create a maze and the child loses sight of mom.

The child suddenly realizes she is lost and panics (adrenaline is released) because mother is not in sight. In that instant, the child recognizes that she is totally alone, lost, and helpless. It is an overwhelming feeling.

Suddenly, her future flashes before her, she has no one and does not know how to go about reuniting with mom. Panic sets in. Muscle tension may be experienced in her stomach, throat, heart, lungs, shoulders, etc., that is likely to be triggered later in life when a feeling of rejection or loss of connection is experienced.

The fear invoked in the child in that single second is way out of proportion to the reality of the situation because mom is just on the other side of the clothing rack. Once the child calls out in fear, mom comes to the rescue, *but* the trauma did occur and might be registered in her muscles for years to come.

Her "Heart Intelligence" connects to her muscles and transmits the same fear level and release of hormones that she experienced during that childhood traumatic moment.

Later in life, the child cannot cognitively connect the momentary childhood department store fear to the body sensations that are being triggered by a present-day situation that also evokes in her a loss of connection to an important person. However, the anxiety stirred up later in life can be mind stopping for her nonetheless.

This is not to imply adults do not suffer significant traumas that will create tremendous triggers for them post-traumatically: spousal abuse, car accidents, assaults, ongoing emotional abuse, bullying, oppression, rape, fire, murder of a loved one, burglary, witnessing violent acts, flood, military combat, and the list goes on.

The difference is that the adult *may* be able to tie their fear to an experience and understand why they feel anxious.

Anxiety

Let fear be a counselor, not a jailer

—Tony Robbins—

Anxiety is a state of being. There are varying degrees of anxiety; however, in all cases, the feeling of anxiety needs to be isolated for what it is—it is a "feeling" or "reaction." You feel anxious—nothing more and nothing less. The sky is not going to fall in. You are in a present situation experiencing an old fear. Let your fear "counsel" your self-awareness.

How should you deal with your awareness of these bodily signals speaking to you and seeking your counsel? The anxiousness is replicating a strong past reaction in you, but the reality of your present moment usually does not indicate an event of such magnitude.

If faced with this situation, you should simply appreciate what is happening, recognize the anxious feeling, and understand that something is being stirred within you. Let the reality of your triggered fear "counsel" your reaction. What in the present moment may be setting off alarms?

Take a deep cleansing breath and trust yourself to work through the feelings. Turn into, embrace, and give value to your feelings—do not turn away from them. That would be avoidance. This is an opportunity to move through uncomfortable feelings and get to the other side of them.

Anxious feelings in present moments that are triggered by past life experiences, consciously or unconsciously remembered, likely bear some degree of resemblance to the present situation.

Similar situations, smells, lights, sounds, environments, or stimuli that mimic past experiences can evoke the release of the stress hormones and bring back similar levels of childhood emotions that attach to the unrelated current situation.

Most of the time, your in-the-moment anxiety is not based on reality, and there is not an imminent threat. You are simply feeling anxious because old fears are being replayed. This is the commonly shared reoccurring response to past fears.

Having anxiety does not mean there is anything wrong with you. Anxiety only means that you are feeling unsettled, apprehensive, or fearful about a situation. Usually the anxious feeling is out of proportion to what reality warrants. It can be dealt with. Reframing your viewpoints can become your means to resolution.

However, if a traumatic event occurred at one point in your life that was life threatening, very dangerous, or harmful, the level of anxiety you may experience merely by leaving your home, can be paralyzing.

If this extreme level of intensity has been your experience, I caringly recommend seeking professional intervention to address that level of fear. Treatment for PTSD (post-traumatic stress disorder) would be appropriate. The traumatic event needs to be cognitively and emotionally processed, and that requires professional help.

In very simple terms taken from the article, "Post Traumatic Stress Disorder: What Happens in the Brain?" published in the "Journal of the Washington Academy of Sciences" fall

2007 edition, the brain temporarily disconnects its visual part from its feeling part during a trauma.

The separation of the visual cortex (found within the cerebral cortex area of the brain) from the emotional processing part of the brain (the limbic system found within the cerebrum) functions to act as a protective mechanism.

The separation occurs because the event is too horrendous emotionally for the individual to attach a verbal description to what they are seeing and experiencing during the traumatic moment. Also, the brain during trauma recognizes its first order of business is to get the person out of the traumatic situation in order to survive—so emotions have to be postponed until later.

Survival becomes the focus and the memory of the situation gets walled off in a remote storage area of the brain (the amygdala) that becomes inaccessible to our conscious mind.

The brain creates a level of dissociation between the cerebral cortex, where visual processing occurs, and the cerebrum, where emotional processing happens.

The brain walls off the event in the amygdala, not allowing the person access to the memory in the present or the future. Consequently, the event cannot be remembered let alone processed and worked through. It is likely the symptoms of PTSD may result.

According to the book by Ogden, Minton, & Pain, *Trauma and the Body*, the amygdala is instrumental in the function of "sounding the alarm." However, during an event threatening enough to cause PTSD, the amygdala can become injured, losing its elasticity to go back and forth between calm and arousal—perpetuating ongoing generalized anxiety.

In other words, the amygdala becomes stuck in the heightened state of awareness mode creating on-going generalized anxiety.

For the individual experiencing a severe trauma, putting words to what they are seeing would elicit emotions in the moment they cannot handle adequately. Furthermore, their focus during a traumatic event must be on survival and how to fix it NOW—in that exact moment—not to figure out what it all means.

However, later on, the visual memories may be replayed in nightmares or flashbacks that the person is unable to account for or understand because the memory has been walled off. PTSD can also induce the tendency to sleep walk.

Throughout this book, I insert experiences from my life to demonstrate a real-life example of the topic or situation being discussed to humanize the point and bring the context to life—here I offer such an example: once I outgrew my crib, I habitually walked in my sleep.

The brain's two processing centers, the cerebral cortex, where visual processing occurs, and the cerebrum, where emotional processing happens, need to be reconnected following the traumatic event in order for the trauma to be properly worked through so that the fear can be understood, and put into perspective—all of which will reduce or relieve recurring and seemingly unexplainable anxiety.

Without professional intervention, the two separated brain functions surrounding the traumatic event can remain dissociated for years or even the remainder of a person's life.

Because the event has been walled off in the memory bank of the amygdala, the individual cannot functionally recall the event to even know it needs dealing with. The need is determined because of their present behaviors and/or anxiety. Please consider professional services if you think you may be dealing with any level of these symptoms.

As explained in the same "Journal of the Washington Academy of Sciences" article:

During their emotional development, if the child completes normal integration of their mental templates, then they can endure a lot of physical and mental attacks and not lose their identity. They will develop their particular strategies for survival.

If however the trauma is severe enough, then depending upon the trauma and when it occurred, one or more particular templates may remain incomplete; they do not integrate.

Sadly, the child does not know this has occurred. The painful future, the misunderstandings to come, the failures and confusions, these will all make little sense to them.

They think that their brain is operating the same way that everyone else's brain does. They think they have the same genetic templates and the same completed personality. They do not understand why they have problems.

What this excerpt is saying is that significant trauma, either from a single event or accumulated trauma from ongoing environmental factors, interferes with the developmental stages (templates) of emotional growth.

This might prevent the adult person from being able to integrate their different needs or emotions from a unified whole perspective and that will yield them challenged in their ability to see reality and be able to reason and sort through their confusion. His or her mind is bouncing between different perspectives stemming from fear and they cannot perform executive functions efficiently.

The stress created by that confusion stimulates the adrenal glands to release cortisol. Because of the hormone levels released, it can feel overwhelming and paralyzing—creating a generalized fear that keeps those hormones levels elevated throughout life.

The generalized stress and muscle tension induced from the elevated hormone levels can create a continuous muscle tension throughout the body and over the years that may lead to significant health and job performance concerns. Becoming self-aware of your stress hormone levels could help you to offset similar future issues.

Sensory Processing Disorders are recognized by the National Center for Learning Disorders as being linked to childhood developmental delays. (https://www.ncld.org)

> Auditory, Visual, and Sensory processing disorders are widely recognized as cofactors for children with developmental delays.   https://www.brainbalancecenters.com/who-we-help/processing-disorders/ If the brain cannot properly process the auditory, visual, and sensory information it receives, a child's ability to learn and thrive in an academic setting is affected, often leading to low self-esteem and social withdrawal.

Trauma also can be experienced by the ongoing repetition of a situation (i.e., being shut into a room repeatedly) or by environmental situations that might not be considered to be a threat. For example, accumulated trauma can result from a child living in an environment where emotional needs are not adequately met on a daily basis due to things like a self-absorbed parent, alcohol in the home, depression in a caregiver, or a harsh parent. (There is a difference between a harsh parent and a firm parent.)

These circumstances can all contribute to an insecure environment. If an environment does not feel secure or safe, it lacks stability. Generalized anxiety can develop out of unstable environments.

In homes where schedules are extremely tight, there is little time for relationship building and connection. Workloads can be so demanding that the work schedules are frequently given the priority and the children live in a whirlwind. All of these situations can contribute to ongoing accumulated tensions and fears.

Living in an environment where the parent is present but is simply not engaged with the child's needs can feel like abandonment. This is an example of an ongoing environmental situation that does not nurture the child; such an environment may lead that child to perceive and believe they are not worthy of love.

A non-nurturing environment where the parent is withdrawn and depressed may cause a child to assume the role of the parent. When that happens, the child will likely take on the role of being responsible for their parent's happiness at the cost of overlooking their own needs.

The child may also take on the role of parent to any younger children in the home as well. In both of these cases, the child has been parentified and loses out on the freedoms of childhood.

My Experience: Connecting My Adult Anxiety to a Childhood Trauma

A significant purpose in setting out to write this book is to help you recognize and acknowledge the presence of anxiety within you as well as to help you understand how anxiety may have developed and allow you to begin to validate your emotions. My purpose is also to convey to you that you are not alone.

I have presented many different situations and environments that can contribute to the development of anxiety and that are likely to continue throughout life.

The purpose in presenting this discussion on some of the sources of anxiety is to enable you to find a match or a similar circumstance from your past that provides a plausible explanation for your stress and validates the feelings you struggle with. You need to recognize the presence of anxiety through your symptoms. If you do not develop the ability to recognize tension in your body so you can work with it, you will likely to remain its prisoner.

I share my path to discovery with you in hopes that my story will ignite a spark or register a similarity with your feelings that may cause you to begin to actively pursue your story. This is where you can begin to harness those emotions and use them to take action.

I go into personal detail for the purpose of illustration. My objective is to add clarity to the context through illustration and perhaps my illustrations will stay imprinted in your mind longer than the educational material presented throughout. Attaching a visual image to the content may bring my words to life in your mind.

When I first entered therapy, I had no clue that I was suffering from generalized anxiety. If someone had suggested that, I would have laughed. I just thought I was quiet and easy-going. I thought I was easy-going because I rarely reacted to anything.

I was unknowingly too afraid to react and, instead, kept everything battened down, bottled up, and secure from exposure. That effort created ongoing, underlying tension within me.

> *Find out who you are and
> do it on purpose.*
>
> —Dolly Parton—

Through therapy, I began to understand my calm was really an unconscious cover-up. All I knew was that I was an intense person, similar to a duck that looks calm and smooth on the surface of the pond, but underneath its feet are paddling madly. I knew that I had always been tense, but I never would have attached a word, such as "fear" or "anxiety," to my overall tension.

I could not understand the origins of my tension or stress so I turned to books to help make sense of it all. I read *The Anxiety and Phobia Workbook*, by Dr. Edmund Bourne, which encouraged the reader to identify some type of past trauma. I could not think of anything—I thought I had had a normal childhood.

Continuing to search, read, and work with *The Anxiety and Phobia Workbook* caused stories that I had heard growing up to begin to enter my mind. But I tended to dismiss them because I had no cognitive memory connected to those stories. The stories did not elicit any feelings inside of me. It was like the stories were about someone else—not me.

However, an auditory memory of one story in particular echoed more strongly within me and I began to think that story might be my plausible traumatic event—perhaps that story was a significant key to my puzzle.

I decided to explore it.

I remembered hearing about a two-week hospitalization for the treatment of encephalitis that I underwent when I was 18 months old. Apparently doctors told my parents that no one was allowed to visit me at the hospital during those two weeks because it would be too upsetting for me to see them leave after each visit.

I also remembered hearing about how despondent I was when I was finally brought home from the hospital. My mother regularly told and retold the story about how I had refused to look her in the eyes after my return home—I would turn my face away from her. She said that continued for many months. While this was a story about me, internally I heard it as a story about someone else, not me. I was not able to connect to it.

I began to consider that perhaps that was my trauma. I certainly had no cognitive memory of that hospital experience, but the pieces began to fit together. I asked my mother about that story and got verification that that story was about me.

She related her experience of coming to the hospital with my sister and brother, and they hid behind some furniture outside of my hospital room where they could view me through windows into the nursery, but I would not be able to see them.

She described me, sitting in a high chair, and stated that I looked dead. She said there was no life in my body or face, and that it was terrible for her because I had been such a gregarious baby. She also said that the nurses had taken away any bottle, as well as my baby blanket for fear of infection.

I started to understand that the feelings of abandonment that I must have experienced in the hospital 45 years earlier were connected to what I was feeling in 1997 when I was alone at home while my husband and children were gone for work or school.

In reality, even though my mother and family had not left me forever, as an 18-month-old, I had not known their separation from me would be temporary. I think I must have thought I was not wanted or I was unworthy of their love. I could begin to feel the shame and despair that I believe I felt in 1952.

I connected the impact of that pseudo-abandonment from that early hospital experience to my feelings of abandonment in 1997, and began to understand those were the same feelings being triggered that Fall because I had been left alone again by my family. I was reliving the feelings of rejection and shame as if it was a traumatic reenactment of the original event.

The connection between my adult feelings with those from my early childhood experience was a huge discovery. I do not think I could have made that discovery without the help of therapy. What I had gone through as a baby was surfacing 45 years later.

That scenario registers with my heart. The feeling of shame was all encompassing. I had never been cognizant of my shame, but over time, I have come to know that shame has always been a predominant motivator in all my decision-making and behavioral tendencies.

WOW—things began to make sense. My feelings of rejection and shame became my core story.

It was at this point that I could begin to believe that my tension and stress were true anxiety. Dr. Brown explained I had generalized and social anxiety, meaning that I lived with varying degrees of anxiety all the time, heightened anxiety in social situations and elevations in those levels of anxiety depending upon what was happening in particular moments throughout my days.

Understanding that my body was experiencing stress and tension was the first step on my journey. I hadn't known that my stress and tension were connected to anxiety. I hadn't known I had anxiety, and I certainly had no awareness of the childhood trauma that triggered the anxiety. The only thing that was true and certain for me in the beginning was that my body felt tense all the time.

Coming to understand ourselves more completely is where we must all begin in order to set ourselves free. Assembling this collection of information that I have studied, tested, and proven works is my gift to you. I believe you can gradually implement this plan to resurrect your life.

Whatever level of body sensations and muscle memory you experience, these are the sensations that you need to begin to recognize for what they are. Embrace whatever information you may discover, name it, honor it, accept it, and work with that knowledge.

Not owning what you discover will only perpetuate your current levels of stress. Did wanting to deal with your stress and tension motivate you to buy this book? Are you looking for peace and confidence? This is your opportunity to begin that process. If you do not recognize these body sensations through self-awareness, you will not be able to move toward more control over your tensions as well as bring more peace into your days.

You need to believe you have the ability to control those sensations and bring them back into balance. If unattended to, they will overturn your day and perpetuate the release of cortisol and adrenaline contributing to unstable health.

Consider your stress and tension to be the gift that leads you to knowing it is time for change and a healthier life.

This is all about **mindset** and I believe you have the ability to create that mindset. I know you will transform your life as you develop a scouring mindset focused on finding the hundreds of opportunities that pop into your path everyday. I will be so eager to hear about your success.

It is important to be self-aware to learn why you do the things that you do. Self-awareness is the process of having a clear perception of your personality, including your strengths and weaknesses, thoughts, beliefs, motivations and emotions.

—Psychefacts.com—

Chapter Wrap-up

You are embarking on a journey to resolve a universal problem—the problem of anxiety—that you have in common with people around the world. Mental chatter reflects cognitive dissonance and you can learn to harness it.

Anxiety manifests itself physically in many places in the body. Anxiety can even manifest itself in muscle memory. The examples and circumstances from my life that I provide throughout this book are offered as an example to illustrate ways in which anxiety might be playing out in your life.

Understanding how life's events, even from your childhood, impact your present life helps to validate what you feel and begins to let you see a way to work through your anxious feelings, accept that those feelings do not represent today's reality, and allow you to begin to harness and transform them into peace and confidence ultimately allowing you to "let them go."

Becoming self-aware of the muscle tension in your body is the first step you must take on this journey to taking back control of your life.

Your Action Plan

Begin to implement self-awareness of the muscle tension throughout your body. The muscle tension is your mind's cue to take action. Changing your brain requires establishing new neural pathways that will form from all the new interpretations that your reframing will begin to accrue.

> Perform regularly spaced body scans at various times throughout your day to cognitively register how frequently you are holding onto tension in your muscles. You may even want to set a soft alarm on your phone to give you six different reminders throughout the day to get yourself in the habit of doing these body scans.

> Use the Symptoms of Anxiety table in this chapter as a guide when you are doing your body scans.

> Be sure to check your shoulders, your jaw, and whether you are using shallow or abdominal breathing—these are all indicators of tension.

> At this point, simply register the presence and frequency of stress—that is what is important at this time.

Dig into the next chapter to discover how the subconscious mind creates thinking traps that our conscious mind needs to become aware of in order to foster new energy and allow us to shift negative thinking into positive habits.

Chapter 4

Our Beautiful Minds

*If the human brain were so simple
that we could understand it, we
would be so simple that we couldn't.*

—Emerson M. Pugh—

This chapter briefly summarizes choice theory and the theory of multiplicity, two theories concerning how our tremendously intricate minds function. The understanding of these two theories will play a large role in your recognition and acceptance of your ability to create change in your life. Remember—you are your most valuable resource for creating that needed change.

Choice Theory

Choice theory, developed by Dr. William Glasser, contends that humans choose "everything" they do, including the misery they feel. In his book, *Choice Theory: A New Psychology of Personal Freedom*, Glasser contended people *subconsciously* choose to feel miserable, sad, helpless, or stuck, to name a few.

People tend to *subconsciously* decide that they are used to feeling a certain way and do not explore the possibility of change. They would rather stay where they are because doing otherwise stirs a fear in them. People are busy and it feels stressful to think about change. The thought of dealing with something new feels uncomfortable. People like their comfort zones. According to choice theory, not doing anything is, in reality, a decision or choice to do nothing.

I am so excited to introduce choice theory to you because plugging this into your thinking process opens so much possibility in every aspect of your moving toward un-leashing your tension.

Success and comfort don't live on the same street.

—Lisa Nichols—

Your choice to change the stress in your life means you will be giving up comfortable and familiar routines and habits that compose a great deal of your day and provide you with stability. Ask yourself, "Do I like living with tension? Is there another side to life where I could be playful and spontaneous? What is standing in my way?"

Glasser developed choice theory because he believed that good, healthy relationships are essential to a happy and prosperous life. He wanted to demonstrate to individuals and couples that how they choose to behave toward each other determines the health of their bond.

He believed that relationships where people choose to work hard together and work at their jobs allows them to feel productive and grow together in a very healthy connection.

He believed people could choose to make their relationship their highest priority over their personal desires. Choice theory is a cognitive way in which to teach people the power they possess in determining their own destiny.

Glasser believed humans need to be aware of the choices they make and how those choices affect those they are in relationships with. In other words, how do your personal choices that attend to your needs affect those around you? He taught his clients to understand how they can change past choices and take more control of their futures. People's in-the-moment choices are what will guide their futures.

> *Everything in life is a reflection of a choice you have made. If you want a different result, make a different choice.*
>
> —Unknown—

Glasser taught his clients to frame the way they lived, acted, and did things by selecting the verb "choosing" and then combining it with the infinitive form of the verb or action (the "to" form), e.g., choosing to eat, choosing to be alone, choosing to argue.

This demonstrates the primary choice theory premise: you are choosing either consciously or subconsciously what you are doing or feeling, thus through self-awareness, you are capable and able to select something better and/or different.

Let's look at an example adapted from Glasser's book. Take someone who describes herself as *being depressed*.

> Glasser taught that person to begin with the word "choosing" and to change *"being depressed"* to its infinitive form, "to be depressed." Describing her self, using the phrase, "I am choosing to be depressed," demonstrates the potential control she possesses, thus allowing her to understand how, and believe that she can, turn her life around. The "choosing to" implies there is more than one choice to select from and that inherently gives the client a greater feeling of control.

You can "choose to" be depressed or you can "choose to" do some other action: visit a friend, go for a walk, or think an **alternate thought** to modify your perception, all of which can make things better by introducing change. As Glasser pointed out, choosing to be depressed does not elicit change; it elicits a downward spiral of more of the same feeling.

Dr. Glasser attempts to demonstrate to the patient that they can have an impact on their feelings through the awareness of "Choice Theory." Depression is by no means a symptom that can just be easily turned around or turned off, however, dealing with recovery from depression can be augmented and better understood with cognitive awareness.

Granted, mental awareness of what you are choosing moment-by-moment needs to be a continuous effort in order for it to become your norm. Slipping back into "being depressed" will occur if the mental awareness of choice theory and the cognition of your ability to select an in-the-moment choice lapses.

But, the client has been given a tool and the awareness of what she is thinking—and of the fact that it is a choice—which can bring hope and new direction into her life. Tremendous perseverance will be needed, but as gradual control over the depression is achieved, it will perpetuate a more permanent change in her emotional stability because she will understand she has the knowledge and ability to change it.

Without this basic awareness of information to initiate change, change cannot happen. The challenge then becomes striving for continuous mental awareness so that a new habit can be created. Awareness leads to change.

You have brains in your head.
You have feet in your shoes.
You can steer yourself any
direction you choose.

—Dr. Seuss—

You have "chosen to" read this book in the hope of learning a method from which to get more control over your stress. I hope you continue, "to choose" to keep reading so that the reframing tools and your new practice of *awareness* will bring you the possibility of change.

Multiplicity Theory

I am multitudes.

—Walt Whitman—

"Multiplicity" is a term used by professionals in the mental health field to describe the ranges of thinking that are connected with a person's various emotional feelings or "Parts."

"Parts" is the term selected for use by Dr. Richard Schwartz who developed the IFS (Internal Family Systems) Model for clinical therapy to help patients understand that the human mind is composed of numerous sub-personalities, all of which exist internally in the individual as the person's "internal family system." In most cases, the voices in each of our heads are our "Parts" talking to us and to each other — they are our "multitudes" or sub-personalities.

In his book, *Internal Family Systems Therapy*, Schwartz states every person has numerous "Parts" or sub-personalities. His theory identifies different functions that our "Parts" play when they speak for — and to us — throughout the day.

He has coined names for our sub personalities based on the various identified functions of the "Parts." They are the "Managers," the "Protectors," and the "Exiles." At the center of all the "Parts" or sub-personalities is our authentic adult part he calls the "Self."

Through years of therapy with clients, Schwartz pieced together similar references made by clients in attempting to explain how their central core feels a certain way. Many of his clients would describe this core as "self" in similar terms, like "my self," "my true self," and "my core self," all referring to the person's center or "Self."

As explained in his book, *Internal Family Systems Therapy*:

> "Self" is the active leader who helps the internal family system (IFS) continuously reorganize to relate more harmoniously with each other. For example, the "Self" may comfort and soothe frightened or sad "Parts," calm raging defender "Parts," or get striving achiever "Parts" to compromise with "Parts" that are in need of more relaxation. In this sense, the person's "Self" becomes the therapist to their internal family system.

*Become an investigator of
who you are.*

—Albert Einstein—

You can recognize and identify your adult "Self" because it is the core of you that experiences emotions, caring for others, empathy, insightfulness, and unwavering confidence in knowing what direction you wish to proceed. Your non-adult "Parts" will be the ones that are fearful, doubtful, angry, driven, or hurt, to describe a few. They will be detectable when your mental chatter is present or even small levels of doubt, confusion or turmoil are felt.

In his book, *The Mosaic Mind*, Schwartz stated that the core "Self" acts independently, yet at the same time, supports the various "Parts" by presenting their needs to the external world. The "Self" is your most precious resource and is capable of leading you from a centered, confident, and compassionate place.

You always want to lead yourself with the core "Self" because the core "Self" possesses "bravery, compassion and curiosity, and projects completeness, truth, and unity," as explained in *The Mosaic Mind*. All these attributes are essential for optimum functionality.

Schwartz maintains that the core "Self "may be hidden behind layers of defensive mechanisms, but that it is always present. The "Self" is competent, a born leader, and supplies you with the capability to preserve healthy function and tie together all your "Parts," all of which together make up your internal family system. Your "Parts" step into and out of the dominant position throughout the day without your being aware of that happening.

Back tracking several paragraphs and taking a closer look at Schwartz's different IFS members, the "Manager" functions by taking control and leading you to be productive, efficient, educated, competent, smart, and likable. Your "Manager Part" functions to keep you steady and not weakened by insecurities. The "Manager" pretty much handles your daily life.

Schwartz describes "Parts" that function to "protect" you from the consciousness of a past hurt or pain as your "Protector Parts." "Protector Parts" can be numerous in number and each one may find a different way of protecting you through various means of distraction.

The distraction keeps you from being connected with a past hurt, creating a buffer or protective activity that grabs your focus. Some of those "Parts" might display a take-charge personality, or escape through an exercising- or adventure-seeking persona. There are too many "Protector Part" types to describe them all and they are individualized within each one of us.

Schwartz identifies one "Protector Part" in particular as the "Firefighter" who emerges when a current situation is beginning to destabilize your inner "family system" with confusion and turmoil (stress), which in turn, sounds the firefighter's alarm.

When the "Firefighter's" alarm is triggered, the "Firefighter" sometimes acts like a bully or tyrant or relentlessly pursues a particular course of action in order to take charge and end inner confusion or fear.

That distracts you from remembering an original experience or emotional pain. By becoming the fearless "Firefighter"— unyielding in its purpose—it provides you with a temporary resolution to the original situation while keeping your focus away from what has caused the alarm to sound.

For example, an aggressive "Firefighter" may be attempting to offset your childlike feeling of helplessness. By inflicting a hurtful comment or acting like a bully, the "Firefighter" gains control of a dialogue or situation and that can empower you, which in turn, distracts and keeps your past fear or hurt from consciousness.

Both "Managers" and "Firefighters" function to prevent you from experiencing self-doubt, past emotions or a painful experience. The difference between the two is one manages routine daily happenings while the "Firefighters" put out the emotional flames.

Lastly, the "Exiled Parts" are those "Parts" that you have no cognition of. "Exiles" are normally out of your conscious reach. Schwartz maintains they are the "Part" of you that experienced the original hurt or situation. The "Exiled Part" is your child or inner person who lived through the hurtful experience and now keeps those experiences locked away from your consciousness.

However, it is important to understand that "Exiles" do feel intense emotions such as guilt, shame, sadness, loneliness, rejection, fear, etc., which is what gets triggered in present-day situations. Those are the strong emotional reactions that alarm the "Firefighters" and are the present-day triggers that manifest in you as stress. They are your tip-off that "Exiles" do exist within you.

When a current situation evokes an old emotion, it is the "Firefighter" who steps forward to protect and distract us from becoming aware of that old feeling. The "Firefighter's" function is to shield the "Self" from becoming aware of that particular unhappy event or fearful emotion, which the "Firefighter" believes will be more than the "Self" can handle. The "Firefighter" does not want the "Self" to get overwhelmed by the emotions of the original event.

Case Study

A client of mine, whom I'll call Guenther, struggles with spontaneous outbreaks of anger. When Guenther gets frustrated and impatient with a task, he begins shaking his head, swearing, and sputtering in a rage at the situation and anybody else within hearing distance.

He recognizes his loss of control and feels badly—after the fact; however, he repeats the behavior frequently, feeling unable to control future episodes. Guenther accepted his behavior as "just being who he is" but came to me wanting to change that behavior because it was hurting his relationship with his wife.

Through conversations and exploration, Guenther tied his rage to repeated feelings of inadequacy he experienced when growing up and doing work for his father. His father owned a plumbing and hardware business, and Guenther worked diligently to do a good job and please his father in the business.

However, it never seemed to be good enough. His father would make a nasal sounding, "Nauck!" exclamation, indicating some level of dissatisfaction with Guenther's effort. Guenther could not remember any other type of response coming from his father.

Guenther was able to recall the hurt and anger he had felt as an older boy when his father judged his workmanship as inferior. He also recalls the anger he felt when his father used his belt to discipline him after an adolescent deviant behavior.

As a boy, Guenther felt ashamed, inferior to his older brothers, helpless to ever get his father's approval, frustrated, and unworthy. He was able to see how his rage in the present moment protected and distracted him from feeling those diminishing and self-deprecating thoughts from his past. His rage in present moments provides an outlet for his old anger.

This distraction is successful because his projection of new anger and energy directed toward the present situation blocks and distracts him from the connection to his father's assessment and the pain it caused within him.

In the present situation, his "Firefighter" releases the rage that he must have wanted to express as a child but as a child, could not express. His current frustration triggers his old frustration with his father's unyielding negative assessments.

As an adult, Guenther can express the rage he was unable to previously express as a boy. The old emotions trigger the behavior or response in the present that Guenther might have wanted to express toward his father in the past. Even though the present situation is very different, the intensity of his feelings remains the same.

Guenther continues to work on his rage, and makes progress. He is able to see himself objectively in his raging moments and oust the "Firefighter" in order to bring his adult "Self" into the leadership position quickly.

Guenther is committed to bringing this change into his life regularly and understands it takes time. His focus is on what he wants to become. When he can accept himself completely, stop judging himself and love the parts of himself that cause him shame, he will attain peace.

Schwartz maintains that our authentic "Self" is not usually or consistently in the leadership role. We go into and out of our different "Parts," depending upon which "Part" is triggered into the dominant role at each particular moment. Schwartz refers to this as carrying the "baton."

Casually, you might say, "a part of me wants to scream" or "a part of me feels angry" or another "Part" is attributed with some other verb, emotion, or behavior. But it is exactly that "Part" that you are loosely referring to that constitutes multiplicity in the human brain.

Everybody functions through multiplicity. We all have multiplicity working within us to varying degrees. Knowing this fact may begin to allow you to view other people's sudden or highly reactionary behaviors as clues to their inner dynamics. See if you can catch them happening.

Every human being has these "Parts." Becoming familiar with your "Parts" through self-awareness is helpful to the execution of the reframing technique so that you can begin to recognize which one of your "Parts" is speaking most loudly during an anxiety episode.

Anxiety triggered by situational fear, ignites your mental chatter. Anxiety represents your various "Parts" establishing a hierarchy amongst themselves. The "Parts" are your inner children—your internal family system—vying to perform their functions.

The mental chatter you become aware of is the interplay being worked out in your head as each "Part" works to capture the stage, distract you from past hurt, control the direction of your choices, and carry the "baton," as Schwartz refers to the "Part" that is in the dominant role.

Throughout the remainder of *Reframing Your Viewpoints*, I will use the term "Self" or "Part" frequently to refer to Schwartz's terminology and concept. I will capitalize those words; however, I will refrain from using the quotation marks around Self and Part(s) for simplicity's sake.

*Without self knowledge, without
understanding the working
and functions of his machine,
man cannot be free, he cannot
govern himself and
he will always remain a slave.*

—George Gurdjieff—

Multiplicity in Anxiety

When you become aware of some level of unrest stirring within, take the time to honor the message your body is sending to your brain. Your body is looking to have equilibrium restored, but you cannot accomplish that without recognizing what is going on.

As I stated earlier, anxiety is a feeling—in reality, it is not a life-threatening emotion. Granted, it may feel strong enough to cause you worry, but trying to avoid it, dismiss it, or distract yourself from it will not bring lasting resolution.

Every one of us has suffered some occurrence of anxiety at some point. Most people suffering from episodes of anxiousness usually choose to avoid the situation because it feels too uncomfortable. They perceive that it is easier and safer to avoid something, rather than going into the fight-or-flight mode. But using the reframing technique can replace the fight, flight, or freeze mode by creating a calm view through reality.

Anxiety in early life can begin as mild, occasional episodes. For example, children can experience recurring episodes of separation anxiety, stemming from some type of experienced or perceived fear of separation from home or their important attachment figures, e.g., parents, grandparents, or caregivers.

Separation anxiety can also develop out of the feelings of not being valued or important—that misconception might cause the child to question the love or long-term presence of a caregiver.

As the child grows older, the anxiety disorder can morph into physical symptoms, such as stomach aches, muscle aches, headaches or as an adult experiencing great unrest or discomfort when traveling alone, sleeping in a hotel room, or being asked to do something out of their comfort zone or area of experience.

As adults, anxiety can occur in the body as cardiovascular symptoms, like palpitations, dizziness, or even a gripping restriction in the area of the heart such that the adult perceives they are having a heart attack when, in fact, it is an anxiety attack. In the movie, "Something's Gotta Give," with Jack Nicholson and Diane Keaton, there is a scene in which such an anxiety attack occurs.

Every one of us has emotional Parts that get aroused. Some of those Parts are hurt feeling Parts, angry Parts, fearful Parts, abandoned Parts, abused Parts, ashamed or guilty Parts, scolded Parts, professor Parts, lawyer Parts, judgment Parts, distractor Parts, and the list goes on.

The point is—these Parts or sub-personalities are very normal components of the human mind. It is the acceptance, love, and integration of all of these Parts that will bring you peace.

Schwartz explains that when your emotions get triggered, if the intensity of the mental chatter that takes over your thinking processes is high, or you are reacting in an extreme manner, you can trust that it is one or more of your Parts that are being triggered.

It is a Part of you from your past that has not resolved the emotions that are attached to the past experience. This creates momentary dysfunction. That Part is stuck in its "Core Story" and core stories are internally written when the child has had an unmet need. It is normal for children to have ongoing, self-centered needs. As an emotionally healthy child matures and attains adulthood, they can satisfy their own needs.

Essentially, Schwartz is stating that your child Part has stepped into the dominant role temporarily and is struggling (once again) to resolve its childhood struggle. You can know and trust it is a child-like Part if the strength of the emotion you are experiencing or displaying is disproportional to the reality of the situation at hand.

In other words, if you find yourself feeling helpless, in a rage, wanting to throw something, feeling like you need to break out of jail and your level of anxiety will not allow you to find any amount of calm, it is because one of your child Parts is holding the "baton" and has control.

That Part of you is fighting to assert your past need or protect you from a past injustice or experience—whether or not your current circumstances warrant such a fight.

How to Use the Self

Your Self needs to help that exiled child Part by providing adult leadership to navigate the stressful situation. Your Self needs to provide clear guidance as an example to your child Part as to how to fix the present stress.

Using your adult Self will demonstrate to your child Part the success and effectiveness of being present as an adult and handling a situation calmly. This will provide positive feedback and build trust in your leadership role for the child Part. The child Part can begin to trust and feel cared for by your Self. Ultimately, this can lead to healing your Internal Family System.

The understanding of how multiplicity operates in each of us provides you with a mechanism of control over your choices. Recognizing who is carrying the "baton," affords you insights into your needs and desires and that allows you to manage life based on reality not based on child-like emotions.

The triggered Parts are still children or adolescents—not adults. Your task is to start to become aware of your Parts and learn about each one them. As you become aware of each one of them, you need to acknowledge they exist, understand the emotion they are experiencing, share the emotion with that child Part, and own it. Bring forth your responsible adult Self so that you will clearly see how to lead that particular child Part forward through their turmoil.

It is your adult Self that you will use when reframing. It is your adult Self whom you want to be in charge 100% of the time. Your sub-personalities or Parts organize your subconscious. To reduce anxiety, you need to rely on your *conscious* functioning.

When you learn about reframing in the coming chapters, you will be learning how to practice living in your adult Self, and you will recognize how much more effectively you handle life. When you learn to reframe, you will make the Self the one who is predominantly leading you through your days. Leading from Self—breeds confidence. Confidence comes from knowing who you are, owning what you feel and think, and fully believing in your goodness.

In presenting the IFS theory, my aim is to offer this information as a life-affecting, decision-influencing concept to assist people in their general understanding of how everyone operates and responds to life. People can begin to believe and trust that cognitive change can initiate and perpetuate a self-altering process.

SAMPLE REFRAMING

Writing this book has been an exciting endeavor. The anticipation of sharing the effectiveness of reframing with people around the world fills me with positive energy and hope.

When I finished the rough draft, it was just that—a very rough draft. I knew, as any author recognizes, I would need to put in many hours to bring it up to its present standard. I was feeling very skeptical. I have to admit that looking back at that evening, I wasn't aware that my child Part was carrying the "baton" when I went to bed that night.

And with that child Part dominating my mind, anxiety was starting an invasion. Voices were beginning to chatter, asking and saying things like, "Do I have what it takes to turn my rough draft into a quality product? Do I have the right to speak about what I have learned? People are going to judge me! I still have so much work to do." I was being ambushed by my self-limiting beliefs.

With these voices of doubt starting up, can you guess what also occurred in my mind? You guessed it—during the night while I was sleeping, I started reframing my perceptions of myself, recognizing I was returning to old mindsets and negative core beliefs from my past.

When I woke the next morning, I felt invigorated and energized—both of which I was definitely not feeling the previous evening. When I woke, I trusted myself to accomplish my goal and handle any obstacles that might distract me in the future. Wow, I realized that I had reframed the situation without consciously thinking about it.

Because the reframing process took place while I was sleeping, I do not know which reframing technique I employed or when and how my adult Self showed up, but I was very excited that the reframing had been so automatic.

This is what I am referring to when I claim that reframing is an integral part of who I am now. It is an ingrained subconscious habit. This is an example of the neuroplasticity I referred to in chapter 2, and I report it here in hopes that it motivates you to start to make it your habit too.

After all these years, do I still need to practice self-awareness to assess which Part of me is carrying the "baton?" Not often, because I recognize my Parts quickly.

Whenever I do feel a rising level of unrest I cannot seem to let go of quickly, it is very helpful to have the understanding of the multiplicity theory—it allows me a pathway to work through simple daily turmoil. When I recognize which of my Parts has been triggered, I am reminded of the effectiveness of striving to stay in my adult Part.

I promise beginning to look for multiplicity in yourself and others will unleash many of your frustrations and help you to successfully navigate your important relationships.

Everything that irritates us about others can lead us to an understanding of ourselves

—Carl Jung—

Chapter Wrap-up

Choice theory maintains that all people have a choice in everything they do or feel, from choosing to feel angry to choosing to go to sleep. It is all a choice.

Choice theory provides you with the understanding that you have the ability to *select* how you deal with anxiety and stress. Choice theory demonstrates how you can "choose" your way into another state of mind. Self-awareness is the first step needed so that you can "choose" your way out of anxiety.

Multiplicity contends that each individual is composed of various sub-personalities or Parts. You have your core Self as well as other Parts that often contend for the leadership role, to carry the "baton" for you.

Self-awareness of these other Parts and what triggers each of them into controlling and launching you into a state of anxiety is an important first step on your discovery path. Through the practice of reframing, you will begin to consciously bring forth your core adult Self, to take control and think objectively how to help navigate exiled child Parts out of states of anxiety.

This book is packed full of information. The new concepts may seem confusing at this point, but as we journey together, you will begin to see how they build upon each other and where to employ them in your reframing practice.

Your Action Plan

Continue regularly tracking the tension in your body using self-awareness and try to increase the speed at which you recognize when it is taking over. When you detect some tension, release it with deep breathing and attempt to determine what Part of you has been triggered and is carrying the "baton."

Chapter 5 will begin to introduce the building-block strategies of mindfulness and visual imagery, which are tools to initiate stress reduction. They can be used as very effective, stand-alone, stress-reducing strategies. In this book, they are also used in conjunction with your reframing practice.

How Does Mindfulness Fit In?

*If you are present, through
mindfulness practice, you will make a
new discovery every time you visit
a present moment.*

—Thich Nhat Hahn—

Introduction to Mindfulness

Mindfulness and visual imagery are stress lowering strategies that, when employed, instantly begin to reverse the physiological effects activated by the release of adrenal hormones due to stress, tension, or fear.

It is important to combine the discussion of these two strategies within the same chapter because together they form a stand-alone, stress-reducing tool—therefore, chapter 5 is lengthy—you may want to divide the reading into two sections.

Lowering the level of these hormones provides immediate relief from anxiety as well as the prevention of tissue damage in the long term from the accumulative effect of those adrenal hormones on your body. Physiological balancing must occur in your body before calmness can be felt.

You can use them not only when you are feeling stress, but also periodically throughout the day just to clear your mind and take a break. They are both proven methods for generalized stress reduction and I promise you will feel their calming benefit within seconds.

They can be used in conjunction with each other or as individual tools for lowering stress. Using these strategies as frequently as possible throughout your day promotes your comfort and skill in their execution, thereby increasing the likelihood of them becoming an automatic method you can use for stress reduction.

The mindfulness and visual imagery strategies presented in this chapter, as well as the self-awareness strategy presented in chapter 6, constitute our three key building-block strategies. With these building-block strategies you are assembling a full armament with which to prevent stress and anxiety from controlling your days. When you employ one of these strategies in conjunction with a reframing technique, you will be unstoppable!

Before diving into the strategies, let's take a moment to honor your individuality. I encourage you to allow yourself to go slowly, take plenty of breaks, and repeat sections, exercises, or whole chapters. Please give yourself permission to go at your own rate and in your own style with the process and strategies you are learning about in this book.

Some readers will see results come more quickly than others. This is not a race, but an evolution—a process. The important matter here is to work through this book at the rate that is appropriate for you!

If we practice mindfulness, we always have a place to be when we are afraid.

—Thich Nhat Hahn—

STRATEGY 1—MINDFULNESS

Mindfulness is used to clear clutter and distraction from the mind so that you can be fully present in a single moment in time. Mindfulness is a building-block skill that can be used to initiate any change you choose to create going forward in life, whether it is reframing or any other goal you may wish to pursue or habit you wish to instill.

Initially, using mindfulness will allow your body to relax and your mind to clear so that you can open yourself to living in the present moment and not be thinking about what you need to do next or what relational issue you are concerned about.

The first objective is simply to learn what it feels like to be relaxed. Following that objective, mindfulness will gradually lead to self-awareness and discovery. Mindfulness leading to self-awareness, as I'm sure you've already gathered, is enormously important in so many areas of your life!

Your muscles need to learn what they feel like when they are in a relaxed state. Here is an explanation of how to practice mindfulness and deep breathing in order to achieve deep relaxation:

1. Find a recliner chair or lie on the floor.
2. Place one hand on your lower abdomen and the other hand below your collarbone on your upper chest.
3. Take a slow deep breath and bring as much air as comfortable into the lower half of your lungs. This will cause the hand on your lower tummy to rise.
4. The hand below your collarbone should remain unchanged.
5. Close your eyes.
6. Take a deep breath and put all your focus on your breath. Mindfulness needs to begin with this deep anchoring breath. By focusing on that first breath, you will immediately let tension out of the body because you will have harnessed your thinking away from your worries

and you will be oxygenating your cells thereby releasing muscle tension.

7. Stay focused on your breathing rhythm. This will keep subsequent thoughts away, clear your mind, and release more tension.

8. Continue to follow your breathing and feel your lower hand rise and fall with each deep breath prolonging your clear state of mind. Sustaining your free state of mind will deepen your degree of relaxation.

9. Try to feel the air passing down your throat and filling your lungs. Trying to feel those sensations helps to keep your mind focused on your breathing and will keep other thoughts from entering your mind. Count to 4 as you fill your lungs, hold onto your inflated lungs for 3-4 seconds and then slowly exhale to the count of 4.

10. Without the distraction of extraneous thoughts, your mind and body will be open to every sensation entering your body. It is in this state of openness that you allow yourself to just BE—no demands, no obligations, no worries, no timelines, and no distractions. The relaxation will continue to deepen.

11. With your focus continuing on the breathing rhythm, the relaxation will continue, and the tension and stress will continue to be eliminated.

12. Try to allow yourself a mindfulness practice of 2–3 minutes. You may even want to set a timer. When you have relaxed successfully for 3 minutes, gradually extend it to 5 minutes.

13. While in your relaxed state, you may or may not experience some thoughts returning, and that is expected. When this happens, bring your attention back to your breath. This is not something to criticize yourself for.

14. The objective is to attain as deep a relaxed state as possible. Feel the weight of your body sink deeper into the chair or floor.

15. Each practice will achieve a slightly deeper degree of relaxation.

16. After you have dedicated 2–3 minutes to this relaxed state, immediately evaluate how you feel—refreshed, relaxed, invigorated, centered, and clear?

17. Then slowly allow yourself to reengage with your surroundings.

18. Go through this exercise 6-10 times on different days striving to get into an even deeper state of relaxation from the preceding efforts. Memorize what your body and mind feel like, then snap a mental picture of yourself—eyes closed, breathing peacefully, and with an overall relaxed feeling in your muscles. Continue to repeat this relaxation exercise regularly, until taking your body to that relaxed state can be achieved spontaneously, simply by initiating a cleansing breath.

19. If you can extend 3 minutes to 5 and then 10, this will yield an even deeper state of relaxation or meditation that you can carry with you for a longer span of time.

20. The next step will be to learn how to focus 100% in the present moment.

It is important to *learn* and *memorize*—both with your mind and muscles—what that deep state of relaxation you have attained through mindfulness practice feels like so that when you take a cleansing breath to restore some calm, you plug in the physical memory of that relaxed muscular state, the mentally relaxed state, and the visual image that you have achieved and memorized. An immediate sense of calm will be conveyed throughout your body.

Combining your breath with the recalled relaxed muscular state eases the tension in your muscles throughout your body, enabling you to begin to restore your physiological equilibrium to move ahead more easily and with clarity in a healthy, balanced direction to successfully employ and proceed more effectively through a reframing technique.

Each subsequent mindfulness practice should bring you to a slightly deeper feeling of restfulness. Each session builds upon the previous session. Keep trying to achieve deeper states of relaxation with each subsequent practice. The goal is to experience the deepest level of relaxation possible. Close your eyes and embrace this new state of being.

There is additional information on mindfulness in the Reframing Exercises and Supplemental Information Packet that is available here: http://bit.ly/ReframeExercise

The Next Step—Present Moment Mindfulness

Let's face facts—few of us have the time during the day to spend lying on the floor and making the effort to go through mindfulness relaxation. We need on-the-spot restoration of calm to reenergize ourselves within seconds. This is where the strategy of present moment mindfulness is valuable.

Present moment mindfulness is the *total* focus on an object or task in the present moment. That *total* focus prevents mental distraction and extraneous thoughts from entering the mind. The total focus provides stress reduction by breaking the pattern of thoughts channeling through the mind and contributing to varying degrees of tension.

Present moment mindfulness is achieved by initiating a deep cleansing breath followed by assigning your focus to one object or task completely without distraction. Stay with that focus for at least 10–15 seconds, and when you return your attention to the business of the day, there will be a renewed level of calm and energy restored.

Go Ahead—Give It a Try

To provide yourself with a quick break during your workday, use mindfulness in this way.

➢ Push your chair away from your desk;

➢ Take a deep cleansing breath to initiate the relaxation response;

➢ Find something within your visual path to focus on and appreciate, for example, a painting, piece of artwork, or a tree outside the window;

> ➢ Focus on your slow, steady inhalations and exhalations while staying mindful and totally focused on appreciating your selected visual object for 10-15 seconds;

> ➢ Slowly reengage with your surroundings while continuing to breath and assess your tension.

In this way, you can achieve a quick, rejuvenating calm.

Understanding Mindfulness

According to the National Institute for the Clinical Application of Behavioral Medicine (NICABM), mindfulness was first taught in India by Buddha about 2,500 years ago to develop full consciousness. In India, the practice is referred to as *sati* and was translated into modern English in 1921. The NICABM claims, "By becoming aware of what is occurring in and around us in a single moment, we can begin to untangle ourselves from our mental preoccupations and unsettling emotions."

The definition I like best for mindfulness is given in the book, *Mindfulness for Beginners: How to Use Mindfulness to Achieve Peace and Happiness in the Present Moment* by Sara Elliott Price. Price defines mindfulness as "the intentional, accepting and non-judgmental focus of one's attention on the emotions, thoughts and sensations occurring in the present moment."

The three components of mindfulness are 1) intentional awareness—pure focus and concentration, 2) non-judgmental focus on all emotions and skill levels, and 3) attention to cognitive processes and bodily sensations occurring within a single moment in time. Mindfulness establishes consciousness of the self.

Every moment we experience is comprised of mental, emotional, and physical components. However, we usually have extraneous thoughts going on in our minds, blocking our attention to total focus, and, therefore, the three components cannot be experienced collectively—we get one or two of the components but not the whole picture.

1) Intentional awareness.

As Thich Nhat Hanh discusses in *The Art of Power*, mindfulness is very simple yet extremely challenging. It requires complete attention to whatever you are doing with your entire being: investing 100% of yourself (full attention) in everything you do.

The 100% attention level means not thinking about the past or the future, but putting all energy completely in the here and now moment. Then follow that minute with the same energy level and attention on into the next minute—and so on. Thich Nhat Hanh wants us to imagine the power of our actions as if each action contained 100% of our focus.

2) Non-judgmental focus on emotions and skills.

Attention to your emotions and the execution of that goal is what your practice of 100% focus should include. That means you should not attach meaning or judgment to your practice. Instead, aim for awareness of what you are doing each minute and register the accompanying emotion with your consciousness.

Allowing judgments to enter your thought stream will interfere with your ability to connect to your emotions, and interfere with the mind-freeing purpose of the tasks. By staying focused on what you are doing each step of the way, and not on how you are doing it or whether you are almost done, will allow potential pleasure to be felt.

Look for and find pleasure in engaging your mind in the total execution and details of what you are doing throughout your day no matter what it is. That will provide you with endless opportunities to practice mindfulness.

Lose yourself in the execution of the tasks. If judgments enter, such as "I hate this" or "This is so boring," that is expected. Simply bring your focus back to the skills needed to perform the task. It is likely you will have to repeat this return to focus many, many times during each exercise. That is OK. It will get easier and you will become more successful.

3) Cognitive processes and body sensations.

Throughout your mindfulness practice the same focus is needed in regard to the particular thoughts that come into your mind and the particular body sensations that occur within your body. It should be like conducting a total mind and body scan in every moment you spend performing your mindfulness practice. Make note of what you sense as a way to learn about yourself.

The point is not to change what you feel, rather to attain self-awareness and acceptance of how anxiety presents itself in you. Self-awareness of where and how stress is held throughout your body provides you with the realization that anxiety is truly affecting you.

Self-awareness of that reality then presents you with a moment of choice: you can choose to offset the anxiety mode when it strikes, or you can choose to continue to let it interfere with your operating in a healthy mode.

Mindfulness as a Precursor to Change

Mindfulness practice *is* the precursor to change. The more consistently you employ the practice, the more habits you will successfully create in your future. Here are two examples of authors that have used mindfulness to initiate changes.

Davina Chessid, in her book *Food Crazy Mind: 5 Simple Steps to Stop Endless Eating and Start a Healthier, Happier Relationship with Food*, shares her efforts of overcoming her obsession with food. She explains how she tried all types of diets and tactics but eventually succeeded by using mindfulness practice.

Chessid gave 100% of her attention to establishing her new habit of mindfulness whenever food cravings hit. When a food craving hit, she used mindfulness to become aware of what her craving (mind/body sensation) was commanding her to do, and took that awareness to cognitively choose to make the healthy choice which brought on feelings of pride and success.

Because mindfulness requires practice, it was not a quick solution, but it did eventually bring permanent change for Chessid because she liked feeling proud and successful rather than feeling the shame her eating habits perpetuated. Her shame led her to more cravings. She too has been successful in creating new neural pathways for controlling her food cravings.

Just as Chessid was able to shed pounds, she also found peace and strength by practicing mindfulness to achieve harmony with her body's true food needs. When you make mindfulness a regular practice in your life, you will become more aware of your opportunities for using the reframing technique that will lead to the peace you seek.

Mindfulness is also suggested for practice in the book, *Hear Your Body Whisper: How to Unlock Your Self-healing Mechanism* by Otakara Klettke. Klettke teaches the reader to apply mindfulness to learn to listen to their body's sensations and messages in order to learn what foods may be causing toxicity within their body.

Aside from beneficial food choices, exercise, an adequate amount of sleep every night, not smoking, and avoiding substance use, I do not think there is anything else that will have as lasting and as positive an impact on your health as utilizing mindfulness as often as possible throughout your daily life to bring you all of the positive health and emotional benefits that can come from regular mindfulness practice.

Mindfulness can be the springboard for all types of desired changes in your life. Clearing your mind so that you can focus on whatever challenge you face will allow you to navigate that challenge in a more peaceful state as well as give you clarity of thought. When you have peace and clarity, you have confidence that will make establishing habits much more successful.

> *Mindfulness is a mental activity that in due course eliminates all suffering.*
>
> —Ayya Khema—

The Benefits of Mindfulness

Let's look at the benefits of mindfulness, what is involved, what is required from you, and how it will impact reframing.

How mindfulness practice will benefit you:

➢ Reduced stress, better physical health, and less muscle tension

➢ Relaxed mental and physical states

➢ Improved mental health

➢ Clarity to sort through the mind clutter to bring resolution

➢ More focus and efficiency in life

➢ Increased interest, desire, and pleasure in doing mundane tasks

➢ Inner peace because you have more control

Reduced Stress and A Relaxed State

You need mindfulness to reduce mental and muscular stress throughout the body in order to initiate a calm and relaxed state. Investing in the time to practice will continue to deepen your level of achieved relaxation and peace. Insights may be blocked when you are not relaxed and open. A relaxed state will open you to understanding and acceptance of new ideas and thoughts.

Improved Mental Health

Most of the time, when people have thoughts, they come in fragments—not complete thoughts and understandings. Mentally, people oppose or challenge their thinking with arguments that interrupt their cognitive decision-making processes. That mental opposition is what is referred to as mental chatter.

Your goal is to take a thought from a beginning point and follow clear steps to reach a new idea, a conclusion, or a final cohesive plan of action that will not be waylaid or compromised by mental chatter. Practicing mindfulness will help you achieve this goal, which in turn will lead to improved mental function and health.

Clarity

Mindfulness clears your thoughts so that learning about yourself without distraction or challenges can occur. Mindfulness will generate clarity. Without the mental stillness elicited through mindfulness, you cannot catch a glimpse of your in-the-moment mental screenshots.

You need mindfulness in order to eliminate your distractions and tune into your "quality world" needs and desires. The phrase "quality world," coined by Dr. Glasser (Choice Theory—chapter 3) will be described in upcoming paragraphs under the heading, Rapid Identification of Triggered Emotions within the section, How Mindfulness Impacts Reframing.

Focus and Efficiency

When you have spent time practicing the building-block skill of mindfulness to become conscious of your Self, your ability to maintain focus throughout your day and not be pulled into a cycle of anxious symptoms will save you time and valuable energy.

You will become mindful of your mental chatter, thus allowing you the ability to choose to restore balance in your thought patterns, make managing your stress your highest priority, and help to attach your focus to the task at hand which will restore efficiency.

Improved Interest, Desire, and Pleasure

Complete, 100% focus introduces you to a new level of *interest* in the detail of everything you do that was previously missing in your life. When you pay attention to the details of the moment, it clears extraneous thinking and resets your balance.

The cognitions gained through mindfulness practice will stir a place within you that may have been numbed, to varying degrees, by life. You may begin to experience simple pleasures again, such as the glory of nature or being captivated by the whimsical childhood pleasure of blowing bubbles.

More Control and Inner Peace

Mindfulness will lead you to the consciousness of how best to invest in yourself, thereby handing you more direction and control. Promoting your own interests is the best investment you can make toward your future and wellbeing.

When you protect yourself and promote your own interests, peace ensues and you feel more in control because you are being proactive in steering your life rather than being reactive and scrambling to fix it.

What is the Objective of Mindfulness

Initially practicing mindfulness will seem awkward and perhaps frivolous. And that is OK since the goal in cultivating mindfulness is to be *unconcerned* or *playful* to whatever arises. You need to be fully accessible to experiencing whatever is happening around you as well as inside of you in that unconcerned moment.

If you are concerned or worried, you cannot be open to the intentional awareness, non-judgmental focus, and the cognitive processes or body sensations that define mindfulness. If you are open, insights will come—gradually.

In general, people rarely sit down to just be alone and think. People sit down to rest while watching TV or listening to music, playing electronic games, or they sit to read a book, magazine, newspaper, or something on the Internet. People sit down to have a snack while multitasking—sending texts and emails. Society considers all of these relaxing.

However, what people need is to unwind, relax, and just "BE" while breathing deeply into that BEING. They need to seek an inner stillness. And that's what mindfulness practice is all about.

Many people, without their being aware of it, are in constant search of distraction. They subconsciously (with the help of their distractor Parts) feel a need to disconnect from their surroundings or emotions, in order to prevent their awareness of inner struggles. Their life is not comfortable unless they are busy doing something and those something's become their subconscious distraction techniques.

Peace: it does not mean to be in a place where there is no noise, trouble, or hard work. It means to be in the midst of those things and still be calm in your heart.

—Unknown—

What Is Required of You?

Let me share a metaphor about mindfulness, so you can gain a greater understanding of the practice. Buddhist Hanh explains mindfulness by using the metaphor of someone having the recognition that they have a beautiful yard and then that person decides to make time to walk around and enjoy their yard. They take a couple of steps, appreciating the nature, colors, flowers, breeze, and "feels of the day," all with good intentions.

However, within several steps around the yard, the preoccupations with their work or relational problems are too strong and distract that person. The total engagement and enjoyment in the wonders of the yard is lost. The desired relaxed state of BEING is lost to the tensions of life.

In order to achieve the level of relaxation and consciousness needed for mindfulness, you will need to practice being mindful. Without the mental stillness prompted with mindfulness, you cannot catch a glimpse of your in-the-moment thoughts—your beautiful yard, so to speak. You need mindfulness in order to clear your distractions so that you can see your triggers and feel your emotions that notify you when you need to reframe your viewpoint of a situation.

A moment's insight is sometimes worth a life's experience.

—Oliver Wendell Holmes, Jr.—

How Mindfulness Impacts Reframing

Mindfulness impacts reframing by allowing you to see, hear, and feel yourself in many different circumstances. Mindfulness will awaken in you an understanding that change is needed. You cannot reframe what you have not seen or felt. Mindfulness clears your mind to become self-aware. Mindfulness practice over time will gradually bring:

> ➢ Efficiency and efficacy in producing a relaxed mindful state so that you are connected to your inner self and can most effectively employ reframing.

> ➢ Inner awareness of your in-the-moment attitudes.

> ➢ Immediate recognition of an arousal in your emotions so that you can address your needs.

> ➢ Rapid identification of which emotions in you are being triggered

Efficiency and Efficacy in Producing a Relaxed Mindful State

Practice generates efficiency and efficacy—in everything.

Inner Awareness of Yourself

Gifting adequate time and openness to your mindfulness practice will connect you with your thoughts (needs), heart (desires), and body (peace or unrest). Mindfulness will open you to understanding on a new level what composes your life. Your breathing awareness can become your anchor in every present moment to help you stay tuned into that inner connection. You will carry less anxious energy to be absorbed by those around you.

Immediate Recognition of Arousal

Mindfulness will bring the tension you live with out of the closet. You will learn how frequently and pervasively tension resides within your domain. Beginning to replace your tension with openness through the practice of mindfulness will allow you to begin to engage with life.

Rapid Identification of Triggered Emotions

We are back to the connection that mindfulness *will* establish between your cognitions and your heart ("Heart

Intelligence"). Mindfulness will gradually allow for and ignite rapid identification of your feelings.

As an illustration, I point again to the time I have spent understanding my fear of abandonment. When I sense that abandonment fear being hooked into (triggered), I can right away associate *why* the present situation is provoking that fear even though the present situation in no way resembles abandonment.

Because I recognize it is not my present reality, I can immediately "let it go" without using reframing. BUT I would not have been able to achieve that spontaneous response if I had not gone through practice after practice and the accumulation of my insights and self-understanding.

Using mindfulness will open you up to understand yourself on a much deeper level. You can begin to discover why you think the way you do and what has shaped your motives, needs, and fears to create your "quality world," as named by Dr. William Glasser, the founder of choice theory.

A "quality world" is composed of "the small personal world, which each person starts to create in his or her memory shortly after birth and continues to modify and adjust throughout life" (Glasser, 1999). It is our attempt to satisfy our basic human needs.

"Quality worlds" are defined as the people we want most to spend time with; the things we want most to experience; and the core beliefs and rules we have established for ourselves that govern much of our behavior. Our "quality worlds" become our lens, the perceptions through which we perceive life. The lenses on our "quality worlds" can *cause* our misperceptions.

Recognition of a More Relaxed You

Mindfulness will lead you to experience a genuine appreciation of yourself—in a state where you are no longer looking for your sense of self-worth from others by turning to them to meet your needs or phantom desires.

I learned of the concept, "phantom desires," through the movie, "The Life of David Gale." In that film Kevin Spacey, playing a college philosophy professor, quotes the Greek philosopher, Demetrius Lacon, explaining to his class, "The fantasy of desire: it's not the '**it**' that you want; it's the '**fantasy**' of '**it**'."

"Desires support fantasies. The moment you get what you desire, you no longer want '**it**'—the fantasy has been extinguished, and you move on to the next fantasy." Your next fantasy becomes your next distractor.

All the external "things," "idols," or other people you think you need to bring you happiness or create the fantasy of who you are striving to be will not meet your needs. They are your "fantasies of desire," which will perpetuate endless future fantasies.

Until at some point, hopefully, you discover you can be content with who you are—right now. Your greatest stress reducer of all will be when you can finally accept yourself— with all your imperfections and idiosyncrasies—and love yourself fully.

What this means is that you need to be looking inward to find your Self, embrace your Self, and accept and appreciate all your attributes and qualities (without judgment) and use that state of recognition and acceptance to fulfill all your own needs and desires. As the title of one of Richard Schwartz's book states, *You Are The One You Have Been Waiting For.*

As you set down this path to total self-acceptance and look inward to your capabilities and strengths, you will find peace and happiness, your family and friends will sense a different energy coming from you. They will not be able to pinpoint it, but they will feel more connected to you because you are more connected to and accepting of yourself.

They will gravitate towards you because they will feel you are not as tense, your energy is more channeled and flowing, and that you are more open to shared dialogue and to fun.

Mindfulness meditation practice isn't about trying to throw ourselves away and become something better. It is about befriending who we are.

—Pema Chodron—

Doing the following exercises will demonstrate what I have been writing about, which ties together the mentally and physically relaxed state that comes from 100% focus. As you read through the following sections, you can start to play with mindfulness.

Take that mindfulness practice into your daily activities to use them as opportunities to practice 100% focus. Jobs such as taking out the garbage or other mundane tasks you undertake throughout your day are excellent chances to insert some mindfulness practice. Focus 100% on, and lose yourself in, the details of the task.

EXERCISE 1: Walking with Mindfulness

Read through this exercise once prior to performing it and understand it is an exercise used to clear your mind by keeping your mind focused on the details of the task.

When walking around your living space, yard, or a park, practice being fully present in every step you take. Notice the details of your movements—how your foot lifts off the floor and goes through the execution of a single step— starting at the heel and rolling through the entire length of the foot, ending that first step by lifting your big toe off the floor as the heel of the other foot simultaneously begins to step onto its heel.

Feel each bone of the foot articulate with the floor. Focus on all the aspects of walking—it does not matter if you go very slowly or clumsily. The purpose of monitoring each foot articulation is to keep your brain engaged in the process of walking throughout the entire 12- to 20-foot walk from one room to another.

See what you learn about balance. Notice where you are placing your feet, how are you breathing (breathing is a wonderful thing to focus on), practice keeping your 100% focus on *any* aspect of the task of walking the 12 to 20 steps.

Your mind needs to stay totally connected to the task. This is a challenge since you will be tempted to think about all the other things going on in your life! (For example, what you need to do later in the day.) Keeping 100% focus keeps your mind clear of chatter.

It does not matter what aspect of the walking you focus on— just focus on anything in that moment except distractions. Where do your eyes look to take you safely from one room to another? Look at what you are seeing as you walk? Keep your mind totally focused on everything that goes into the walking process. Dissecting the walk step-by-step and appreciating the complexity of this task will help you to stay focused.

Experiment by modifying the stepping techniques. Make it fun. Change the walk to a hop or skip or walking on tiptoes. The point is to put your total focus into the action of moving yourself from one room to the next without losing your focus or having your mind wander onto some other aspect of your life.

See what you learn about your ability to focus and what you learn about your muscle groups, balance, attention span, etc. Remember, this is not easy. Do not judge how you are doing or criticize yourself if you get distracted—simply bring your attention back to your breathing and 100% focus on the task.

Finish your short 12- to 20-step walk between rooms. Take a cleansing breath and assess your overall body tension. I predict you will discover that you are more relaxed than when you started. If not, it is probably because you are trying to do the task perfectly, which is not the point of the exercise.

Simply keep focused on the three components (mental, physical, and emotional) that you are experiencing while performing the task, not on how "well" or "poorly" you are performing the task. This gets to the core benefit: it is the sensations and activity of the task that will clear your mind and free you from stress. Ask the perfectionist Part of you to step aside so you more clearly engage in your mindfulness practice.

The total attention to the task will replace fears, doubts, worries, time schedules, and other unrelated issues from your mind while performing the task. Without the stressors in your mind, peacefulness will envelop you. This is the objective of mindfulness. This is the objective of the exercise.

After this exercise, stop and take a deep breath. Do you feel less body stress? Have you totally engaged your mind in the activity, thus eliminating all your worries temporarily (even for a couple of seconds)? Is your muscle tension reduced? Does your mind seem calmer?

These exercises might seem silly, but the benefits will be significant when you get the hang of implementing mindfulness frequently throughout your day. In order to not add more demands to your busy schedule with exercises like this one, you can use mindfulness practice during your regular daily routines, turning those into opportunities for stress reduction in general.

You could focus on your breathing while taking out the garbage or collecting the mail. Mindfulness can be practiced not just when you are feeling anxious but as a general tension reducer throughout your days.

The next time you have a tedious job that you dislike, try turning it into a mindfulness practice—you will be amazed at how using mindfulness changes your attitude and you get through the job so much more quickly.

Instead of wishing you were done with it, take your time and use it as an opportunity to appreciate how well you can focus on and execute the activity. Use that attention to detail to gain mental calmness.

On a note of interest, there are two ceremonial marching companies at the Marine Barracks, Washington, DC. Their primary function is to provide ceremonial support throughout our Capital's region. They train intensely on ceremonial drills and marching. The Marine Barracks, located at the corner of 8th and I Streets in Washington, DC, is the "oldest post of the Corps" in the United States.

If you have ever had the privilege of seeing Company A march or have the opportunity to watch them in the future, focus on how smooth their marching appears. They articulate through every joint in their feet so that it looks as if they are rolling through each step.

When Company A Marines roll through each step, it puts them perfectly in sync with each other because the rolling-through motion sets the pace for their steps so that each step exactly matches all the other marines in the drill.

No other branch of the armed forces accomplishes the smooth, perfectly in-sync rhythm that the Marine Barracks Company A is trained to achieve. They achieve 100% focus during their drills—complete mindfulness—so that they accomplish perfect synchronization. With practice, it becomes automatic through muscle memory. Should you want the opportunity to see the Company A Marines, here is a short 8-minute YouTube video. You will be amazed! https://www.youtube.com/watch?v=AbylW2cKvZM

Whatever the mind can conceive,
it can achieve.

—W. Clement Stone—

EXERCISE 2: Washing the Dishes with Mindfulness

The following exercise can be used as an additional or alternative exercise. Trying each of them at least once would be wonderful. Read through this exercise once prior to performing it.

Doing the dishes with 100% focus.

Things to focus on: feel the soapy water, register the temperature of the water, and ask yourself the following: does the water tend to relax you? Is there any odor coming from the dishpan? Hear and listen to the sloshing of the water. Does it make you feel like you need to pee? Can you smell the dish soap? What does the running water sound like? Is it relaxing? There are many sounds to stay focused on.

Start by washing the glassware because the water is cleanest and hottest when you first begin the washing task. Focus on the wiping action around each glass, rinse with very hot water, and notice how the water sheets off the glassware and the glasses sparkle as you place them to dry.

Next, clean each plate using a circular pattern with your sponge. Notice the bubbles cling and then slip off quickly with the hot water rinse. See the sparkle and shine of the freshly cleaned plate. Finish all the plates and bowls before moving on to the silverware. Stay focused on the process.

Follow with the silverware and notice that it takes more effort to get the forks clean than the knives. Enjoy rinsing away all the soapy water. Is the dishwater getting cold—do you need to add some more hot water to the pan?

Now, have fun with the pans! Notice the heavier food accumulation, rinse or scrap it off, and notice the grease—you will need very hot water to clean away the grease.

If you are drying the dishes by hand, handle each article with kid gloves so that you do not chip or break anything. Take your time—you do not want to stress over broken dishes.

If you are loading a dishwasher, arrange the contents creatively rather than lining them up without much thought. Make sure the dishes are placed into the dishwasher so that they do not clink against each other during the wash cycle. Put 100% effort into the process. The more time you take performing this activity mindfully, the more time you have allowed your mind to be in a restful state. You want to lose yourself in the details of the activity.

Keep your mental process connected 100% with the task. Use your breath as your anchor. That attention to the process of the task should make the job more interesting and more enjoyable because you will be fully engaged—observing and experiencing every aspect of the job—thereby bringing you sustained peace.

The objective is not to see how quickly you can accomplish a task but to appreciate the steps and skills involved in completing the task while acknowledging the sensations that are being evoked from within. It should be a process, not an accomplishment. The accomplishment is in keeping the 100% focus.

Keeping your focus 100% on the activity at hand will keep your mind free from worry or stress, and therefore, the task will be more pleasurable, peaceful, and relaxing.

After finishing the dishes, take a cleansing breath and perform a body and mind scan? Do you feel less muscle tension in your body? Do you feel as if you have had a restful break? When we clear our thoughts, it brings peace and calm to our minds, hearts, and bodies.

These are just two examples of mindfulness practice. It does not matter what activity you select to practice with. The activity is not the objective. The *focus* throughout should be on whatever you are experiencing while performing the activity—looking out the window, washing your hair, brushing your teeth, etc.—focus without distraction is your objective.

If you use these simple tasks as opportunities to practice mindfulness, you will not have to set aside specific times out of your busy day to find practice time. It is exciting for me to think about how much you will benefit from mindfully executing routines around the house—I predict you will agree that 100% focus accomplishes an amazing calmness.

When you wash your hands, when you make a cup of coffee, when you're waiting for the elevator— instead of indulging in thinking, these are all opportunities for being there as a still, alert presence.

—Eckhart Tolle—

How to Practice Mindfulness

I recommend regularly spaced check-ins to glimpse what is composing your thoughts in any particular moment throughout your day—take a *present moment selfie* of your mental cognitions, attitudes, energy level, and emotions. You could do this as often as every 15 minutes, which would provide you with something like time-lapsed imagery.

However frequently you space your check-ins, just keep a tally of what you discover about yourself. If there is a pattern occurring, make note of that. For example, in general do you notice what attitude tends to dominate your mind? Is it a loving or selfish attitude? This is not to be judged—only tallied so you can begin to see *where* change is needed.

Mindfulness check-ins only last a second and are private because whatever you hold in your mind is totally yours and yours alone. No one will be able to detect that you are focused on yourself. No one is privy to what you are thinking, so the practicing can be done without notice by anyone.

Therefore, you can do it frequently throughout the day wherever you like, whenever you like, and as often as you like. HAVE FUN WITH IT! Commit to practicing everyday for one week—practicing at that rate will begin to make it a habit.

Finding Peace

Peace comes from within. Do not seek it without.

—Buddha—

STRATEGY 2—VISUAL IMAGERY

The Cleansing Breath needs to become your **conditioning signal** to trigger an automatic response within your body indicating you are stepping in as an adult to take charge and face a present moment's discomfort.

Calm waits for you on the other side of discomfort—work through it, do not fall back into the old habit of avoidance. The cleansing breath will become your body's cue to switch gears and move forward.

After you have consistently practiced mindfulness daily for a week or two, go back and recall the deepest state of relaxation you attained while practicing mindfulness. Try to physiologically re-capture that same level of relaxation.

If you cannot recall it, go through another mindfulness session to mentally retrieve that relaxed state. If you detect any muscles that still hold some tension, release that tension and reassess how you feel.

Mentally and physically memorize this latest calm state by staying with it for several minutes while continuing to breath deeply—perhaps 2–5 minutes with eyes closed and concentrating only on the in and out flow of your breathing.

After 2–5 minutes, imagine snapping another mental picture of yourself from above while lying with your eyes closed, breathing deeply, and feeling the muscle relaxation throughout your body.

Sustain the mental picture of how you look in that snapshot and lock together the three components (mental picture, physical feeling, and calm, relaxed breathing denoting calm emotions). Hold them together, memorize that picture with the relaxed feeling, and deposit it in your memory bank. In the future, the minute you recall your image, breathing will slow and muscles will relax. This is a powerful tool.

The purpose of uniting the three components of the mindfulness definition (mental, physical, and emotional) is to train your mind and body to physically respond to your mental picture, much like Pavlov's dog experiment on classical conditioning.

Your cleansing breath needs to be like the bell the dogs responded to in Pavlov's experiment—the signal for your mind to recall your mental picture of your relaxed state: cleared mental thoughts, relaxed physical tension, and the calm emotional state you have achieved through mindfulness practice with focused breathing.

It is this relaxed image of yourself that you can mentally recall whenever you initiate your cleansing breath. Linking together the mental snapshot and the relaxed deep breathing whenever you initiate your deep cleansing breath will become your body's cue (like the dog's bell) to recall your visual image that will trigger your stress reduction.

Because of this mental conditioning, the moment you take your first cleansing breath, your muscles will automatically begin to relax and your body will subconsciously begin to restore calm within. This tool will transform your stressful moments as well as set you up to lead from your adult Self.

The visual image is a kind of tripwire for the emotions.

—Diane Ackerman—

You now have two means by which to initiate an instantaneous calming effect: by initiating a cleansing breath or by recalling your peaceful image of yourself. Either of these two stimuli will begin to restore the three components of calm—peaceful mental image, relaxed muscular state, and peaceful emotions derived through the deep breathing. They can be used together or individually depending upon the circumstances.

Do not hurry this process—spend time memorizing how you feel while connecting the three components. The more time you spend holding onto the relaxed image and experiencing the relaxation associated with your image, the more quickly you will be able to recall your relaxed state successfully whenever the need arises.

This is an effective means to handling a stressor. As Dr. Brown told me when I was learning this skill, "You can't go to that relaxed place if you have never been there before." So, be sure to take yourself there—practice.

If you would like to take it up a notch or two, attach an image of a beautiful scene or a significant familiar place that always brings you calm. Pair music with your visual image and/or you can associate emotions, feelings, or sensations to the visual image as well. This can enhance the effectiveness of inducing on-demand relaxation.

While breathing deep, call forth a beautiful scene, feel your body relax, and listen to some peaceful music. Putting the image, music, breathing, and relaxed muscular state together may take you to an even deeper relaxed state.

Stay with this effort to fully make the connection—maybe 15 to 20 minutes (put the music on repeat) and make sure to stay with your breathing. Stay with it to own it and embrace your new feeling of calm.

Eventually, simply initiating 1 to 2 deep breaths when you are sensing stress will automatically pull out the entire "artillery" simultaneously. Your visual imagery will bring an immediate bodily response within you. This is a significant accomplishment. Celebrate this—you have created an effective strategy. Woo Hoo!!!

EXAMPLE OF VISUAL IMAGERY

As a child going to yearly pediatric appointments, I panicked at the sight of needles. I would cry and carry on extensively. As that child in the pediatric office, I was not able to connect my panicked feeling to anything—it just occurred—I made quite a scene in the doctor's office. Vaccinations were a trauma to me and, I am sure, to my mother as well.

Fortunately, we outgrow the need for vaccinations. As I aged and only periodically needed blood draws or tetanus shots, etc., I learned to deal with needles by disassociating from the procedure (numbing through disassociation is a typical PTSD method of coping), which allowed me to *act* like an adult.

I no longer use numbing as my coping method because I am now so much more connected to my feelings, have confidence in my ability to handle my fear, and choose to use visual imagery and reframing, both which allow me to be mindfully present, calm and in control of my cognitive thinking and decision making. I do not want *to choose* a childlike coping mechanism to handle my fears.

When you are in control and calm, you create positive energy and move forward through uncomfortable moments with success and feelings of accomplishment.

While hospitalized in 2015 for cancer treatment and having the more recent understanding of my hospital trauma from when I was 18 months old, I could understand why I was feeling panicked at the sight of needles and why I was feeling angry every time the nurses came into my room to deliver a shot or flush tubing.

The original needle phobia and emotions produced during the two-week hospitalization in 1952 had been resurrected by my 2015 hospitalization experience.

This is an example of how our history can impact our current experiences. Now, whenever I get blood tests, injections, or have my chemo port flushed, my body tenses all over as I anticipate the panic feeling at the prospect of the needle, and I can feel anger rise within me even when there is no current circumstance provoking me to anger.

The visual imagery I rely on to get me calmly through my needle anxiety is the scene from the movie, "Message in a Bottle," where Garrett and Teresa are sailing on the Chesapeake Bay.

I also associate the musical theme from that movie scene to calm my anxiety and the anger produced by the anticipation of the needle. I have taken it up another notch by attaching the sensations of peacefulness that I experienced during my adolescence when sailing as a camper in Maine on the Penobscot Bay.

I recall hearing the rhythmic lapping of the waves on the hull of the sailboat, feeling the warmth of the sun penetrating and soothing my body, seeing the sun sparkling on the water like crystal facets, and feeling the wind blowing over the side of the boat—my hair in a freestyle dance. In those moments, I felt wonderfully free, at peace, and connected with nature.

Retrieving that state of relaxation by initiating two deep breaths is an effective method for defusing my fears. My relaxed body, mental replay of the musical theme, and the visual and tactile sensations I attach to the image elicit an instant mental peace and muscle relaxation in me that I can hold onto while the needle punctures my skin.

This trained behavior has tremendous power over my nervous system. I know you will create an image that has a similar effect upon you. Even if you are only able to recall a shortened version of this conditioning, I promise it will create a break in your cycle of stress, which will allow you to call forth your adult Self. With calmness and leadership you will harness your fears.

Let's look at how you can pair the visual imagery strategy with the reframing technique to create a powerful support method for helping yourself when you start to detect fear or are overwhelmed with extreme stress, anxiety, and tension.

When facing needles and feeling my anger begin to rise, I take a deep cleansing breath making sure I fill my lower abdomen and hold that inhalation for a couple of seconds while adding my visual imagery to initiate my calming. Start this process a minute or so before the actual moment of stress so that you have enough time to get it in place prior to the difficult moments. After a couple of breaths and holding onto my imagery I add **alternate thoughts** such as:

> ➤ These needles are going to give us the information we need to move forward in the ongoing care of my cancer.

> ➤ This nurse is here to help me.

> ➤ This nurse was not present 64 years ago—she has nothing to do with my anger today.

> ➤ The injection discomfort only lasts a nanosecond.

In this way I actively and consciously reframe my perspective of the situation, which results in a significant reduction in my apprehension and anger.

SAMPLE REFRAMING

Let's say you fear air travel, your vacation is approaching, and you will be flying to Hawaii for a two-week vacation. Let's couple the visual imagery technique with the "Going to the SPA" variation of reframing to achieve calm, peace, and control in this example.

See the fear—it might be the closeness of people in proximity to you, the TSA personnel, air turbulence, navigating airport terminals, the possibility of crashing, or something else, like lack of control, crowds, or simply being away from home that makes you fear air travel. Explore that fear—allow yourself the time to focus on it and **See** it. Does it have a color or velocity?

Pheel the muscle tension, sweat, the knot in your stomach, and your increased heart rate due to the fear and anxiety that is being created every time you start to anticipate the vacation. Record how the fear and anxiety manifest in your body—such as increased heart rate or shaking?

Assess the intensity: 9

Take your cleansing breath and bring up your practiced relaxed state and visual image. Breathe again. Ask your adult Self to help lead you to a more peaceful place as you anticipate your vacation.

Assess the intensity again: 8 (You can feel help is on the way.)

Alternate thoughts to be substituted:

> ➤ I will trust the pilots because they have over 20,000 hours of flight experience logged into their flight logs even before they are hired.

> The pilots are updated yearly on their safety procedures and go through yearly simulator training as required by the FAA.

> I am not traveling alone. I will be sitting next to my spouse or travel partner.

> My seat is toward the front of the plane where the turbulence is less.

> I will bring calming music to listen to with my ear buds.

> I will buy a glass of wine or beer.

> I will pack some light snacks, like cheese, crackers, and sliced fruit.

> Talking with my spouse will help to provide comfort and distraction.

> I will hold my spouse or partner's hand.

> I will mentally picture we are boarded on a touring bus, and if there are bumps, I will recognize the bumps (reframed) are only "potholes" in the road while I take some deep breaths.

> I will close my eyes, hear music, and visualize myself seated on a bus (not a plane) next to my partner, enjoying a snack and wine.

> I will hold onto these images every time I begin to anticipate the upcoming trip.

> I will envision the beauty of Hawaii and the wonderful activities we will share together.

Assess the intensity again: it is down to a 4 or 5

If you practice this combination of tools every time you fly, the newly reduced tension you feel can become your new (greatly decreased) level of travel apprehension. Each trip will provide you with a new experience by which to gradually reset your level of apprehension to a lower and lower level.

Every subsequent trip will elicit less stress than the one before. In chapter 9, this type of gradual exposure to more positive experiences will be presented in a discussion about exposure therapy.

Peace is not something you wish for: it's something you make, something you do, something you are, and something you give away.

—John Lennon—

Chapter Wrap-up

Mindfulness will become your new close friend as you embark on this reframing journey. There are so many ways in which it can benefit you both physically and emotionally. As stated previously, mindfulness can be the key to initiating change in anything you dream of achieving.

Your stress-reducing artillery is now four-strong. It includes recognizing you have a choice to reduce tension, bringing forth your adult Self, and using mindfulness and/or visual imagery. The sequential engagement of this offensive weaponry will begin to rebalance your hormone levels. We are building a strategic plan of action.

Your Action Plan

Create your visual image, pair it with your deepest relaxed state, and, if you like, pair it with music. Make a plan for implementing mindfulness and visual imagery practice throughout your days.

> Remember, it only requires seconds of your time—you just need to be aware of when the opportunity to insert it arises.

> Consider setting alarms on your mobile phone to remind yourself to practice mindfulness or visual imagery at specific points throughout the day even just to take a mental break.

- ➤ The more frequently you practice, the more benefit you will feel.

- ➤ Five to ten minutes of mindfulness every night before bedtime can help to relax you and make falling asleep quicker, and your quality of sleep will probably be deeper.

- ➤ Attend traditional yoga classes—they will focus on breathing and that will help with relaxation and mindfulness. Hot yoga or power yoga most likely will not promote the relaxation focus of traditional yoga.

Download the Reframing Exercises and Supplemental Information Packet that contains more helpful information on mindfulness: http://bit.ly/ReframeExercise

Chapter 6 digs into the importance of self-awareness and the necessity of using self-awareness for creating new habits in life. Chapter 6 is key to transforming stress and anxiety into peace and confidence. The information is Chapter 6 will affect every aspect of your life.

Let's Explore Self-Awareness

*It takes courage
to grow up and become
who you really are.*

—e. e. cummings—

Self-awareness, the third of our eight strategies, comes as a benefit of mindfulness. It is an offshoot of mindfulness because it is your cleared and focused mind that will allow you to notice something about yourself. To be self-aware means to be conscious of your thoughts, energy, attitude, traits, feelings, and behaviors.

It is self-awareness that you need in order to recognize you are in *need* of a reframing moment. If you are not aware of an increasing level of stress, then those hormones triggered by stress are continuing to circulate throughout your body. Recognizing your tension level through self-awareness provides you with the opportunity to take back control and protect your body against the harmful effects of stress.

Employing self-awareness throughout the day will benefit you in every aspect of your life. You must have the awareness of a problem before you can initiate change. This book is giving you an opportunity to learn a valuable skill that will reach far beyond the reframing technique. Let's get started.

STRATEGY 3—SELF-AWARENESS

Before you can do anything about stress and anxiety, you must first become aware that stressors are taking over your emotional state. Self-awareness means noting or identifying to yourself those instances when you feel a stirring inside that says something like:

> ➢ Watch out.

> ➢ How do I respond to this?

> ➢ I am not sure how I feel about this.

> ➢ Give me a minute.

> ➢ I don't like what I am feeling.

> ➢ I am irritated.

> ➢ I am confused.

> ➢ I am angry.

> ➢ I feel uneasy (uncomfortable or on-the-spot).

> ➢ Something isn't quite right here.

Your greatest challenge will be *remembering* to check in with yourself to become self-aware. The more regularly you take note of the signs of stress, the more sensitized to them you will become. Remember, the signs of stress are your FRIENDS trying to help you—they are your biofeedback mechanism and internal barometer.

Self-awareness is what alerts you to the body's warning signs that are being delivered throughout your body and begging for you to notice that stress and anxiety are creeping in. Tune into your body's warning signs and give them the attention they deserve.

Previously, you may have felt the discomfort of the warning signs but plowed them out of the way without giving them much regard. We try to flee unrest by being in a hurry or using distractors or avoidance tactics. Fleeing anxiety can be accomplished by:

➢ Ending the conversation

➢ Putting off a response

➢ Remaining silent (which sends the message that you are in agreement)

➢ Changing the subject

➢ Venting or blaming someone else

➢ Distracting things away from the subject to avoid it completely

➢ Distracting yourself with an unrelated activity or chasing fantasies—the "fantasy of desire"

➢ Phone calling or connecting to people in order to keep busy

➢ Watching TV, playing on the Internet, exercising, eating, or engaging with social media

All of these tactics only temporarily postpone or dodge the real issue at hand. The underlying reason for the stress will come back to ruminate and haunt you at some point, causing you to have self-doubt, turmoil, and/or loss of sleep. You may think avoidance protects you when, in fact, avoidance keeps you imprisoned in fear.

Reframing your perceptions will gradually allow you to see the repetition of the same fears playing out again and again. The fact that the same fears continue to cause you unrest, frequently and in different situations, provides you with evidence that you *need* to have a method by which to gradually disempower them.

When you become aware of any one of the potential feelings listed above as a warning sign, just make note of it. You need not judge the existence of the anxiety; only recognize its presence quickly as part of your self-awareness practice.

Self-awareness allows you to make a tally sheet of circumstances that cause anxiety. The tally of circumstances will cause you to understand the frequency and, therefore, the *need* to alleviate stress from your life in general in order to safeguard your health.

*The mind's first step
to self-awareness must
be through the body.*

—Dr. George Sheehan—

Recognizing symptoms more quickly will allow you to have better control over the effects of stress on your physical and mental health. Fine-tune your self-awareness to red flag any of these reactions so that you can attend to them.

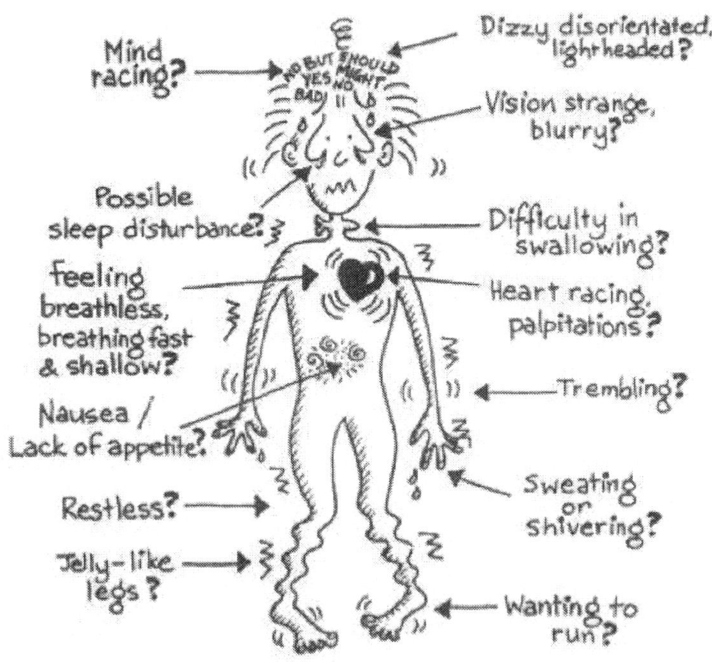

Image from straightpathtorecovery.com

As with mindfulness practice, you can practice self-awareness not only when you feel some unrest but also in regularly spaced check-ins that you perform on yourself every hour or at the frequency you select throughout the day.

This self-awareness practice of regularly spaced body scans, to search for various symptoms such as muscle tension, clenched teeth, racing mind, or restlessness, will establish the frequency of your underlying stress. You might be surprised at what these body scans reveal.

Things you might observe include-in-the moment attitudes; inviting or avoiding dynamism; feeling sadness or joy; feeling fatigue or energy; or feeling anger or restlessness. You learn about who you are through self-awareness. The frequent check-in routine provides you with an ongoing picture of your attitudes. For example, are your love channels open (adult Self) or are you focused on childhood needs or losses?

Getting to know yourself in this way may seem burdensome and unnecessary, but it increases your self knowledge, which I have emphasized, is necessary for your optimum success at restoring peace and confidence in your life as time goes on.

As established in chapter 3, anxiety is not unusual. It is an unsettled feeling or apprehension about a situation that can arise frequently and to fluctuating degrees. Anxiety is not a feeling to fear—only a feeling that you will learn how to better manage. The feeling is something to *appreciate*, as it is your body talking to you to let you know you are in a stressful mode. Your body is simply asking you to please return it to its healthy equilibrium.

Once you have established the correlation between the awareness of your body's stressful warning signs and the understanding that you can very quickly initiate action to reduce the stress, you can capture that awareness and take it to the next step: harness the stress and cognitively "choose to reduce" that stress or anxiety level by reframing your viewpoint.

We cannot alter, change, or redirect something of which we are not aware. Therefore, the establishment of every new habit, like choosing to reduce stress via reframing, requires the initial awareness of the problem in the first place. So we are back again to mindfulness, self-awareness, and the relevant overlap of those skills.

When you are practicing self-awareness and notice that you feel some anxiety, make note of the intensity. If you can discern the reasons for the anxiety, put them aside to return to shortly, because the reasons do not change the feeling. You simply need to recognize the anxious feeling and label it—*I am feeling anxious*—take ownership of it. You will learn that many different circumstances elicit the same physiological response.

Objective Self-Awareness

> *Self-awareness involves deep personal honesty. It comes from asking and answering hard questions.*
>
> —Steven Covey—

Objective self-awareness invites you to be your own observer. It requires you to allow vulnerability and imperfection to be identified as part of who you are. We all have vulnerabilities and imperfections—perfection is an elusive objective and is never possible. You need to see yourself from the outside looking in.

It takes stepping outside of yourself to assess the "micro-communications" of every situation. It asks you to assess how the other person is interpreting the situation and how they are feeling.

Micro-communications are the underlying energies, like body language, facial expression, or posture that are present during every personal exchange. The nuances of expression, tone, or verbiage are also micro-communications. Objective self-awareness can be equated to watching a movie of yourself where you can see and detect the subtleties underlying the dynamics between people.

Others see what you show them. To some degree, we all wear a public mask. We have an inner concept of what we believe we are and what we want other people to believe us to be. Objective self-awareness will allow you to be the observer of yourself to learn how accurately you achieve that image.

By observing yourself objectively from an adult perspective, you will be able to evaluate whether other people are seeing what you want them to see and whether, in fact, you are projecting the desired image you thought you were working hard to project.

When we hold anxiety either in our tone of voice or body language, people can sense it, and they often interpret it as anger at them rather than a fear you are internalizing.

Frequently, when other people sense your anxiety, they respond in kind, meaning they will absorb that energy and then both of you may feel anxious. So what you have is a communication between two "Protectors" as explained in chapter 4 in the section about multiplicity.

If you feel some tension at the beginning of a communication or for some reason you are not comfortable, one of your "Protector Parts" may be carrying the "baton," as coined by Dr. Schwartz, to label the Part that is in charge at any given moment.

When your "Protector" is in control, it's tension energy may be absorbed by the other person—putting the other person on guard and alerting their "Protector" of a potential threatening situation.

So, now the conversation might be occurring between two "Protector" sub-personalities, both of which are not adults. The ensuing conversation will likely not be very successful. The anxiety coming from both of you may sabotage the interaction, distorting it and negatively affecting the outcome.

Objective self-awareness can allow you to see, in a mindful/self-awareness moment, how your own body language may be interpreted and how the other person is responding to it. By observing how you are perceived, you can alter your body language or posture within that moment.

If you were self-aware of your tension when starting to engage with an individual and, therefore, had initiated a cleansing breath to reduce your tension, taken a self-awareness moment, and chosen to bring forth your adult Self, the whole interaction would play out much more comfortably and productively.

The professional journal, "Psychology Today," states that 55% of communication is body language, 38% is tone of voice, and 7% is the actual wording.

Therefore, checking in with yourself, using mindfulness and self-awareness in a single moment before or during a conversation, may tip you off as to the type of energy you are contributing to the interchange.

Another way of looking at this is that if you sense that someone is anxious, agitated, etc., in a conversation with you, then consider whether that person may simply be reflecting the anxiety you may be communicating to them through your own body language, tone of voice, etc., or whether the other person is the one bringing the anxiety to the interaction.

If it seems the negative energy is coming from the other person, take a deep cleansing breath, ask your adult Self to step forward, hear what is stirring in them and open yourself to working together toward the same goal.

Allow yourself to see the situation as an opportunity for connection rather than conflict—and that would be reframing. Instead of debate—relate. If needed, step away for a minute to give everyone a moment to reflect and then resume the talk.

Once you have a realistic understanding of how people perceive you, you can consciously adjust your presentation to match how you want to be perceived. The dynamics of communication are critical to your success in your family, work, social circles, and community environments.

Learning to become consistently self-aware is the most important aspect of any goal setting you ever want to achieve. This strategy will be life changing.

SAMPLE REFRAMING

Contemporary Behavior Therapy, by Michael Spiegler and David Guevremont provides this excellent example of reframing that I paraphrase below:

A 44-year-old woman, who worked at the same company for 12 years, decided to leave her job at the end of the year because her supervisor was forever criticizing her and she hated going to work each day.

The woman felt good about her decision to leave, but she was finding it increasingly more difficult to put in her last weeks there. It became a terrible drudgery to get in her car and drive to work every morning because she hated thinking about the number of days she still had left to work there. She felt on edge her entire way to work and felt resentful and stressed throughout the day because of her supervisor.

This woman could **see** her *anger* toward her supervisor and her *fear* of the supervisor's criticism. She could **pheel** the humiliation every time the supervisor chastised her, especially in front of other employees. She was living in fear of even being near her supervisor.

She rated her intensity level at 8 or 9.

Using a reframing technique, this woman substituted the words "anger" and "fear" with the word "appreciated" as her **alternate thought. She now "appreciated" the frequent criticisms from her supervisor because it validated her decision to leave the company.** Rather than trying to avoid this woman, she set her mind to envisioning the supervisor's comments as a "pat on her back" for her decision to leave.

She was able to inwardly celebrate that decision every time her supervisor began to go off on her. Every day, she left work crossing off one more day until she would be completely free of that person.

She continued to use her **alternate thought** during her last weeks every time the supervisor started in on her—the woman began to actually feel positive energy toward her supervisor instead of anger. She actually began to inwardly smile and rejoice because she knew she had taken back control.

Her final day at the job was coming and she could focus on what lay ahead. Instead of wishing she could change her supervisor or somehow get revenge—both of which were not realistic or appropriate and would have kept her spinning with inner turmoil—she could become energized by where she was headed.

Now driving to work, her stomach was no longer tied in a knot, and her days could be enjoyed with the co-workers who were her friends. If she had not reframed her anger and fear to reflect appreciation, she would have continued to live with her stress symptoms throughout her last weeks at that job.

She rated her intensity level at 1.

A Celebrity's Tool

Tony Robbins has trained his mind to reframe his perspective in 90 seconds. He has trained his mind to instantaneously recognize tension in his body. Once he catches onto his mental state, he understands his mind has taken over and it is filling him with sadness, anger or frustration. He slows down, (cleansing breath) acknowledges what he is feeling, then immediately finds something in the situation or moment that he can appreciate, love or be grateful for (present moment mindfulness).

Because our minds are not capable of holding onto two different patterns of thought at the same time, he chooses a dominant mindset and successfully changes his negative frame of mind to positive.

Chapter Wrap-up

Mindfulness is a significant precursor to your gaining self-awareness. The information gained and evaluated through self-awareness can be key to your finding peace. Practicing mindfulness so you can insert self-awareness is extremely important to how quickly you become comfortable and spontaneous with the mindfulness and self-awareness skills—both of which are fundamental and necessary to initiating change. They can become automatic over time.

By now, you have a picture as to how these skills are interrelated and understand they need to be practiced with habit-forming attention, so you do not lose either time nor momentum in learning how to reframe your viewpoints.

Your Action Plan

> ➤ Tune into your stressful situations throughout your day—do not avoid them—use them to identify your triggered emotions. You do not need to feel pressure to reframe them at this point.

> ➤ Keep a mental tally of the triggered emotions and name them.

> ➤ Spend time thinking where those emotions come from.

> ➤ Look for words that disempower their intensity.

➤ Journaling your mindfulness practice can increase your skills and provide evidence of your progress.

➤ Question if you are staying stuck versus moving forward?

➤ Examine your attitudes: are you in a loving mode or a wanting mode?

Set up a 90-day commitment to starting to use these skills and strategies earnestly and consistently. This will provide you with the ability to measure how your life has been altered at the end of the ninety days, thereby allowing you to accurately measure my projections.

Chapter 7 provides the rationale for gaining insight and understanding of your own emotions and behaviors that will ultimately turn reframing, as a technique you practice, into reframing—your automatic habit.

What Else is Needed?

*Chance favors the prepared mind.
The more you practice, the luckier
you become.*

—Richard Branson—

Insightfulness, the fourth strategy of the eight, will come gradually as you practice mindfulness and self-awareness. Everything is interrelated. The more you are mindful, leading to increased self-awareness throughout the day, the more quickly you will gain the insights to understand the what, why, and how you think and behave the way you do.

STRATEGY 4—INSIGHTFULNESS

Gaining an understanding of what types of situations trigger your stress and anxiety will lead you to recognize which emotion is being hooked into, and that will lead to your ability to more quickly choose an **alternate thought** when you employ a reframing technique.

Gaining insight means you begin to recognize that your anxious feelings are generated from past experiences. You may be able to connect a feeling with a specific memory. This connection may not occur quickly. It may take time with repeated efforts at trying to sort through confusion or "areas of gray."

Let me give a brief overview of how to attain insightfulness: following your next awareness of a stressful feeling, allow yourself the time to explore that feeling of anxiety and identify it. When you do connect to a tension, stress, or anxiety, ask yourself—looking into your heart—"What am I feeling?"

Place your hand over your heart. Then wait quietly, breathing deeply and without distraction for your answer. It will come at some point. Stay with that question and open your heart to whatever possibility may surface. It may be a very tiny voice or fleeting thought but listen to it, trust its authenticity, and explore it.

Spend time sitting with that question and remain receptive to whatever voice you hear or feel in your heart. If and when you become aware of a response from within yourself to your question, determine if it resonates with your heart. Sit with it a bit longer and allow yourself time to measure its truth. This will be your "Heart Intelligence."

> *Be still—be quiet—and then you*
> *will begin to see*
> *with the eyes of the Heart.*
>
> —Desmond Tutu—

If you are able to gain some understanding of which past experiences connect with certain feelings, continue to explore as many of those as you can. Perhaps you can ask your parents, caregivers, or extended family members about certain memories in order to validate those memories and gain some additional information, perspective, or knowledge.

Taking the time to journal or keep a running list of your insights and your core beliefs will allow you to go back to them and explore them further. See the repetition of how often they show up and any patterns or how regularly they play out in your viewpoints and interpretations.

I want to share with you some of the insights that I have gained about myself over the years because I believe they are similar to the core beliefs that many of us share in common and I offer them as an example of what I am encouraging you to discover about yourself.

I have learned to understand that when I am feeling stress, tension, and anxiety, it is often because I am 1) judging myself; 2) making what others are thinking or wanting more important than what I need; 3) putting my voice on hold because I perceive their voices as more worthy than mine; 4) assigning my needs, desires, and opinions a lower priority in relation to everybody else's; or 5) feeling responsible for everyone else's happiness or validation; 6) I may be feeling rejection or a strong need for validation and significance.

I continue to see those old beliefs and motives resurrected in some instances where I feel my stress levels rising. BUT, what I want you to understand is that because I have identified this list of negative core beliefs, I can immediately associate which one or two are being triggered and understand that those beliefs are a part of who I am—but in my present life, they do not serve me well. They have no value to me because they are not based on reality. I do not want to spend my valuable time rehashing what I have already disproven through all my efforts over the years.

If you are not gaining insights into the origin of your anxiety, please consider seeking professional assistance. You will get to know yourself, attach meaning to your feelings, and accept and integrate all your valuable Parts that are within you.

You can come home to "Self" as Schwartz identifies in the book, You Are the One You Have Been Waiting For. I even recommend working with an IFS (Internal Family Systems) counselor. You can visit http://www.selfleadership.org to locate a practitioner near to you.

Be patient with yourself. This is an opportunity to be curious in this learning and discovery experience. Travel through your history to try to associate a time when you may have experienced some gain in self-understanding that leads to your feeling calmer and more centered. You are not trying to find Parts of you to eliminate. You want to harness these Parts to use them in a productive way.

If you have previously experienced feelings of unrest, those feelings can come from very different situations than what is causing them in the present situation. However, the angst in the present moment is strong and keeping you from healthy functioning in that moment.

For example, rejection can be an underlying fear brought on by something from the past, like the physical absence of a caregiver, the emotional absence of a caregiver, rejection on the playground when repeatedly being the last one chosen to be on a team, or the death of a parent or caregiver before you were able to understand that their death was not about something anyone caused, contributed to, or could have prevented.

It just happened, and there was no way to explain it to you in your young state; or perhaps you remember an argument or unrest that occurred between you and that person just prior to their death and you are left feeling guilt and shame.

It is now well established that adoptees feel rejection from the birth mother even though she may never have been present following birth. Bonding with the birth mother occurs during gestation. The gestational bond is psychological, emotional, physical, and chemical.

Normally after birth, the bonding formed during gestation deepens and contributes to the self-love the child needs to establish in order to flourish in its development. However, if the biological mother is never present following the birth, the infant is left with an inner void that fills with self-doubt. Cognitive identification of the void is not usually likely. It can manifest in a combination of disorders.

If the gestational bond is broken after the birthing process, the infant experiences it as loss and rejection—as something was wrong with them—they were not wanted. This is a form of abandonment that produces an underlying trauma without any conscious memory.

As a young teenager, our adopted daughter stated she never "felt satiated," meaning she never felt filled inside— that something more was needed—she was very conscious of feeling a persistent void.

She had continuous overlaying thoughts and questions about her history and the contexts from which she came that generated identity questions and a deep need to discover her background. As reported by her, this deep unrest was her experience of the adoption trauma.

The biological bonding and love is deepened after birth and is reflected in the mother's eyes as she gazes into her baby's eyes. Bonding deepens as the mother holds the baby, and the mother satisfies the physical and emotional needs expressed by the infant/child.

A child's trust continues to develop from the biological attachment. A continuation of the attachment to the biological figure after birth deepens the child's ability to trust in life and build healthy future relationships, thereby allowing for healthy autonomous growth over the years.

Because of the biological break, the abandoned child is likely to grow up with the core belief that they are defective or unworthy; therefore, their mother didn't want them and she left them. It is very personal to the child and the core beliefs they develop because of the relinquishment affect them throughout their life.

Circumstances impact our lives and it is how we feel emotionally about those circumstances that stay with us and become our stories. For our son, the adoption experience influenced his development. He internalized that he was not enough for us—as if he was lacking in some way and that is why we had to adopt. It was the fact that we loved him so much, that we wanted to expand our family.

Gaining insight over time will lead to understanding how and why you think and act in certain ways. The understandings you gain from insightfulness are not to be used to judge yourself. Insightfulness requires time with yourself in which to learn to appreciate who you are—much as parents learn about their children as they grow and develop.

You need to parent yourself: learn about how you think; learn about what makes you feel joy or happiness; learn about how you respond to life—with openness or with fear; learn what hurts your feelings; learn about what causes you to become angry, etc. Then take that knowledge and create a life that nurtures and enriches your inner being. Take the time to pursue those enrichments and make them a high priority.

Gaining insights will take time, but every new insight or understanding contributes to solving your jigsaw puzzle— one piece at a time, with each piece adding some new dimension to the picture. Sometimes the discovery can be unsettling because it may be something you were not aware of.

Please do not judge your discoveries—explore them for more depth if you feel able. If you spend time criticizing yourself, it is time wasted, and your focus will be stuck on the negative instead of where each discovery may lead.

Connect to and learn about yourself in ways that have been blocked and kept hidden away from you by all of your distractions over the years. As Richard Schwartz describes, your "Protectors" have shielded you from feeling the fear, hurt, or anger, which a past traumatic event or an unstable environment may have caused in you. They have worked hard throughout your life at distracting you and keeping you unaware of what you have experienced and felt. Become curious.

*At the center of your being
you have the answer:
you know who you are and
you know what you want.*

—Lao Tzu—

Embrace this learning guide as a way in which to learn how your life experiences shaped your development and constructed the set of core beliefs that you operate from every day.

When you learn about yourself, you begin to appreciate how you have survived this far and understand with compassion what has influenced your development. When you learn about yourself, you can begin to appreciate the wonderfully unique individual you are. Only then can you admire the strengths that you have developed.

From a faith-based perspective, as you learn and grow, you can begin to love yourself as God loves you—unconditional love without judgment. Allowing the acceptance of God's love to fill your heart sets the stage for you to begin to love yourself unconditionally, without restraint, and in earnest so that life can be experienced freely. Begin to frame life through God—His law is Love, His Gospel is Peace.

SAMPLE REFRAMING

You are facing a job interview next week that you want to prepare for. You can't seem to focus on the preparation because you feel overwhelmed with agitation and unrest. You find yourself pacing and unable to focus because the fear about how you should prepare is blocking your clarity and organization. Additionally, your inability to focus on the preparation is adding to your mental chatter.

The fear of showing up for this interview unprepared and being rejected is causing you to panic, and the panic freezes your efforts at preparation. Thus, a vicious cycle is created, and that cycle exacerbates the situation, which elevates your fears, apprehensions, stress levels, and hormone secretion.

Now, imagine that it is a week later. The previous week was not productive for you in terms of preparation. Now, the day before the interview, you try to anticipate all the questions that you may be asked. You draft up a list of possible questions with detailed answers. You spend several hours at the task. You recognize there is no way you can memorize all the written-out responses—more fear sets in.

You think about what you should wear to the interview and take the time to try on a third of your wardrobe as well as practice role-playing with yourself. More fear and self-berating set in because you think you need to be doing more.

STOP ... STOP!

You could practice out a zillion roles, go to the interview, and still altogether miss the focus of how the interviewer ultimately handles the interview. You might have spent the better part of your week or day in angst anticipating and trying to optimize your strategy—but in the end the interview may play out totally differently than how you anticipated it.

A better use of your time and energy would be to use your mindfulness and self-awareness to *identify* when that interview anxiety is taking over and pushing your logic out of reach. With the understanding that you are spinning in anxiety, choose to *harness* it and *transform* it through reframing.

Self-awareness of your mental state is the key to freeing up your mind and taking back control of your day, stabilizing your emotions, reducing your stress, and achieving a level of peace. Your goal is to recognize your familiar anxiety habit and replace it with your new reframing habit. It is a cognitive choice.

Let's go to the SPA

S—See the anxiety

P—Pheel the feeling

A—Alternate thought to be substituted

See the fear. Let's say you have spent several weeks or months practicing your mindfulness habits, so you are now prepared to jump quickly through the SPA process without having to learn about why you have those feelings or where they come from. You recognize that it is your fear of rejection playing out in this interview situation.

Pheel the fear of being rejected. Recognize it and how very scary and paralyzing it is.

Assess your intensity level: 10

All of your practice with the four building-block strategies has brought you to a new place. You know yourself better after the mindfulness practice and know where in your past those feelings of rejection have come from.

You have acknowledged where they were initially or repeatedly experienced or felt, accepted those feelings, owned those feelings, and were brave enough to learn how that must have felt when you were young and originally experienced them.

Because of all your practice, you immediately recognize that it is anxiety being stirred from your fear of possible rejection by the job interviewer. This is a normal anticipatory apprehension for everyone on a job interview. Because of something in your past, that apprehension is far stronger in you.

Take your deep anchoring breath and use your visual imagery to start to restore your physiological equilibrium. The visual imagery will begin to reduce the amount of the adrenal hormones being released, which needs to happen first, so that some level of clarity returns. Success with re-establishing a calm state cannot be successful without pairing it with the physiological balance that will be initiated in your body with your cleansing breath and/or visual imagery. With this new focus, choose which Part of you will lead going forward.

Now you are ready to reframe with your adult Self.

Provide an **alternate thought** based on your adult experiences in life. From your adult perspective, what statements can you offer yourself that will reframe the situation and eliminate or reduce your level of fear? Some examples of **alternate thoughts** you might use to balance your perspective and help you to focus on reality might be:

- ➤ I have done five interviews before and handled all of them quite well. This will be no different.
- ➤ Three out of the five job interviews resulted in job offers.
- ➤ I have the buzzwords and attitude to make a positive impression.
- ➤ I have a great deal to offer this company.
- ➤ I have done research on this company and understand how I can help solve this company's problem.
- ➤ I want to appear authentic.
- ➤ I am a team player. I have the experience stated in the job description that they are looking for and need.
- ➤ Interviewers are friendly, fair, and respectful.
- ➤ Interviewers equally want to provide a good impression of themselves and the company.
- ➤ I have three letters of recommendation, so they can read about my potential and why I would be a good fit.
- ➤ I **need** to interview them—I **want** to meet my professional goals.

Notice how this last statement shifts your viewpoint and energizes you. Notice if one or more of these statements resonates with you, causing a calmness to replace some level of your angst. Now when you think about preparing for your interview, you may have a different view of what your preparation for the interview might look like.

Summing up and combining these thoughts will enable you to more clearly construct an **alternate thought** that might immediately change your perspective and empower you with positive energy. The goal is to transform your fear—negative energy—into positive energy—so that you can move forward. Actually writing your thoughts out on paper is helpful and clarifying.

Alternate thought: I need to interview them—I want to meet my professional goals.

You have taken fear out of the equation and substituted it with goals.

Assess your intensity level: it's a 5.

If your anxiety is still too disturbing, work with or add some other **alternate thoughts** that work better for you and yield positive energy. You get to choose to take control and to choose your words with which to calm yourself. This is why reframing your viewpoints requires you to be in Self. Self will lead you because Self integrates all your Parts, respects their fears, and appreciates their jobs but still says, "Follow me—I will parent you."

Knowing yourself is the beginning
of all wisdom.

—Aristotle—

Chapter Wrap-up

This chapter talked about the value of personal insights in gaining self-understanding. As you continue to practice regular mindfulness and self-awareness, insightful gains will come gradually to you over time. You must remember to be patient and love yourself with this slow unfolding of your story.

Allowing yourself the time to reflect on your discoveries and appreciate how your life experiences have impacted you will create a bond between you and your heart. Look for your subconscious Parts in your path of discovery and take time to sit with them and get to know them. This is an on-going process—if pursued—it will bring you personal growth, self-acceptance, and peace.

Your Action Plan

➢ Keep looking for as many opportunities to practice mindfulness, self-awareness, and insightfulness as possible to propel yourself along the journey to setting yourself free.

➢ You can practice the strategies simultaneously or you can focus on getting comfortable with one at a time before adding the next. Eventually mindfulness, self-awareness, and insightfulness will all blend together.

➢ As I've recommended already, establish set times each day to do quick self check-ins to practice mindfulness, self-awareness, and insightfulness. It can happen inside your mind in just moments—as long as you *pause* to do it!

➢ At one of your check-ins take a few minutes longer to record your practice and findings in a journal. This will lead to your gaining greater insight because you'll be able to review your entries to find patterns, allowing deeper insights to emerge.

➢ Don't judge yourself for the feelings you recognize. Instead, embrace and nurture these feelings. Celebrate your getting to know yourself. Learn what your inner child needs.

➢ Let me know how things are going, ask a question or give me feedback.

Chapter 8 brings the strategies of forgiveness and empathy into the spotlight and examines why those characteristics are so valuable in navigating life.

Connecting to Your Heart

*Your visions will become clear only
when you can look into your own
heart. Who looks outside, dreams;
who looks inside, awakes.*

—Carl Jung—

In this chapter we'll talk about the fifth and sixth strategies: forgiveness and empathy.

Why is forgiveness recognized as a strategy? It is a strategy for forward movement because when you hold onto grudges and don't forgive others or yourself, you maintain negative energy in the form of anger, anxiety, and stress that can pop up and take over frequently and at particularly unwelcome moments.

Negative energy from anger in itself produces body tension. Practicing forgiveness will contribute to freeing yourself from that anger, anxiety, and stress that is anchoring you to the past.

Similar to the forgiveness strategy, the empathy strategy asks you to have empathy in your relationship with yourself as well as in your relationships with others. Empathic understanding equalizes relationships and fosters growth between people. Employing empathy toward others strengthens the desired bond, dissolves boundaries, and allows for true sharing— thereby reducing tension.

STRATEGY 5—FORGIVENESS

Forgiveness is something that each of us needs to extend toward others as well as toward our own selves. By not forgiving yourself for poor past choices, behaviors, academic performance, not loving your neighbor, etc., you convict yourself and continue to be the judge and jury, repeatedly inflicting an injustice upon yourself.

By judging yourself and not forgiving yourself for being human, you continue to perpetuate self-criticism. Rejection that may be felt as a child can morph into rejection of yourself. You are not accepting yourself—you are too busy wishing you were different from what you are. You keep yourself stuck in the role that you have judged to be unacceptable and that perpetuates a cycle of hopelessness, stress, and anxiety!

It is time to say goodbye to all that.

For personal indiscretions inflicted upon us, most people believe that reconciliation needs to take place so that forgiveness can follow. In fact, the reverse is true.

Reconciliation cannot begin until forgiveness has been extended and accepted. According to Sidney and Suzanne Simon in their book *Forgiveness: How to Make Peace With Your Past and Get On With Your Life*:

> ➢ Forgiveness is not forgetting.
> ➢ Forgiveness is not reconciling.
> ➢ Forgiveness is not condoning.
> ➢ Forgiveness is not a feeling; it is a decision.
> ➢ Forgiveness is not just about the person who hurt you.
> ➢ Forgiveness is not absolution.
> ➢ Forgiveness is not self-sacrifice.
> ➢ Forgiveness is not a clear-cut, one-time decision.

The Simons also point out in their book what forgiveness is:

- ➤ Forgiveness is an internal process.
- ➤ Forgiveness is a sign of positive self-esteem.
- ➤ Forgiveness is moving on.
- ➤ Forgiveness is about letting go of anger.
- ➤ Forgiveness is about letting go of vengeance.
- ➤ Forgiveness is something you do for you and toward you.

Think of some small personal indiscretions that people have either intentionally or unintentionally inflicted on you and use them as practice forgiveness situations. When you have worked through small indiscretions, you can graduate to more substantial hurts.

Acts of violence that cause us bodily harm or emotional trauma usually must be worked through extensively before forgiveness can possibly be found. You may not be able to forgive a violent perpetrator but you must forgive yourself for not having been able to stop it from happening or for not being able to clear it from your mind.

Choose to stop criticizing and judging yourself. Choosing to love yourself will lead to your choosing to forgive others. Love the part of you that is in the way of your making these choices—it can transform your judgments.

We usually try to get rid of the part that we criticize about ourselves. Getting rid of what you do not like about yourself is not possible; however, you can embrace that part of you and transform it with love.

Make your choice to move ahead. Choose not to be a victim of your self-judgments and choose to break out of those chains. It may seem very difficult to pull yourself out of that familiar victim role because the injuries you have received may have been significant. Feeling like a victim may be very familiar to you because you cannot remember feeling any other way. Therefore, it is comfortable and it has been your norm for many years.

As stated in previous chapters, it is a habit role and you wear it easily. It is like putting on an old pair of shoes that are broken in, and those shoes are your most comfortable pair.

You do not notice the holes on the soles because you never bother to look at their bottoms. It is your favorite pair of shoes, so you continue to wear them until one day you walk through a puddle and water gets inside the shoes. Can you feel the sloshing in your shoes?

Choose to look at the bottom of your shoes and see the holes. Choose to see where your habitual beliefs may represent holes in your thinking. Choose to buy a new pair of shoes, trusting that in time, they too will become equally as comfortable. Choose to change your habit role, so just like with the new shoes—in time, that new habit will also become very comfortable.

In this metaphor between your favorite shoes and choosing to create new habits, know that your new habits will become more comfortable (just like the new shoes) and will provide you with more strength on which to build the foundation you need to take you to the objective you hold for your life—to live without stress, in peace and confidence, and with clarity and optimism.

Think about reframing your history: was there another side to the person/people who injured you? Did they ever treat you in any other manner? Do you remember any times when you felt their love? Were all of their actions selfish? Can you find a memory of a moment where you shared a loving connection? Those people have "multiplicities" like each of us but that does not mean they did not love and adore you.

Your child Part's perspective or Part evolved out of hurt and/ or fear, and that Part will hold onto that perspective until you help it to see reality. Its purpose in your past was to stabilize you, keep you safe, and preserve your self-image. Your child Part still sees that as it's main job—whether or not the circumstances, years later, call for it. You no longer need that type of support. You have grown up but your child Part remains stuck in the past, is unable to mature and continues to pull you back in time.

Our child Parts cannot grow and mature until we love them and parent them and lead them out of their emotional prison.

Look through those bars and see the child that was injured. Are you still a child without recourse? Give yourself permission to unlock those chains and be free. If your child Part continues to dominate, you will not be able to put yourself in a place to practice reframing. You cannot move on to positive changes in life because you are caught in a child-like perspective that struggles to satisfy old unmet needs.

Using compassion, visit your fears, engage with them, and lead them forward to the reality of today. This will allow your child Part to grow up and take on a different function. Therefore, the first order of business in learning reframing is to search your heart and mind, and detect where some judgment or anger at yourself may be hiding.

You will need to forgive yourself for keeping yourself fixed in that victim role for so long. You will need to forgive yourself before you can move freely into the task of reframing life. If you stay trapped in the victim role, the hurt role, the helpless role, the angry role, or the hopeless role, your child Parts are allowed to dominate—and they will continue to replay the old recordings.

Find your negative self-judgments so that internal forgiveness can bring internal reconciliation. Reconciliation allows you to move toward inner harmony and loving yourself, which is your ultimate goal.

Your hurt, negative judgment, or negative self-belief based on past experiences, messages, or behaviors will interfere with your moving through this learning process and finally attaining peace. It is your "Core Story" that needs to be amended and finally given a new ending.

*To remember who you are,
you need to FORGET
what they told you to be.*

—Unknown—

STRATEGY 6—EMPATHY

Empathy is the vicarious experiencing of feelings between two people. The elicited feelings connect you to your own experience while also connecting you to the other person's experience, emotions, and their heart's story. Empathy is something we must learn to extend to ourselves as well as share with others.

Compassion as opposed to empathy is the sympathetic sorrow and concern for the sufferings and misfortunes of others. Compassion does not necessarily establish heart-to-heart connection, whereas empathy does. Empathy is known to increase pro-social behavior.

When your self-awareness brings to your attention an inner feeling triggered by a circumstance, walk in your child Part's shoes and empathize with their experience. Return to some of the feelings that may have surfaced for you while reading this book. Empathize with the effect those feelings may have had on you.

Blocking access to your heart will interfere with your reframing ability because you will not be able to determine what you feel or need. If you cannot access your feelings, creating an effective **alternate thought** that will empower you, define an action, and change your viewpoint will be more difficult.

Just as with mindfulness, self-awareness, and insightfulness—take time getting to know what you have discovered through empathy for yourself. Spending time with an elicited feeling will allow you to identify the feeling, name it, and experience it. As Dr. Phil says, "You have to name it, to claim it."

The time you spend doing this now is an interim step. As a matter of fact, needing to reframe your viewpoints is also an interim step to your freedom. If you lead yourself and stay committed to this comprehensive plan, eventually, reframing will no longer be needed—you will have established your new neural connections.

Empathy in general, does not frequently occur in our society today and without empathy and compassion toward yourself and others, true connection in relationships will not occur. Authentically connecting with people is difficult to accomplish through brief text messages or through social media.

Social media allows us to share photos, fun times, political opinions or jokes, events, and a glimpse of our lives. These provide brief slam/dunk connections. Empathy is not easily shared through social media because the posts are usually admired, laughed at, or congratulated—which are fleeting forms of connection. They accomplish a quickly shared compassionate or celebratory elicitation.

Empathy is necessary in order to sense another's circumstances and learn from what their experiences have taught them. We need to share with them genuinely. Without empathy, there is not deep connection with another person, and that means there is not full connection to your own heart. We unconsciously block connection to our hearts to avoid feelings of sadness, anger, unrest, or hurt. When we go through life without the awareness of our feelings, we cannot fully experience all that life has to offer and that we are entitled to.

Empathy connects feelings stored in your heart to the other person's heart in a sharing and connected moment. Reflect back—has there been a moment when you have felt truly and authentically connected to someone. Empathetic sharing is a gift of peace between two people.

The slam/dunk social media posts are fun and keep people up-to-date and in contact, but those have become the standards for how everyone "should" connect. The pictures convey privileged situations and great successes. The posts on social media misrepresent our daily norms.

That is just not what reality is. Every person is struggling every day to some degree or in some capacity: financially, professionally, relationally, emotionally, physically or spiritually. Life is full of many stresses, which ensures that not a single person is without some problem that needs working through. No one has everything running smoothly 100% of the time.

Unfortunately, social media provides a quick fix and superficial connection. Therefore, society's need for true connection is not satisfied—the need is still present. Hence, we return for the next quick fix because a heart-to-heart connection was not established. Before we know it, we have gobbled up large amounts of time with social media but still do not feel satiated.

Devastatingly, those we are in close proximity to in the present moment and who could provide us with true connection, have lost out to a true connection with us and us to them because of the time we spend on social media.

Frequently it is our family. Are those the connections you want to block? Connections do not have to be verbal—they can be a touch, a hug, or just being together in silence.

Empathy requires us to be aware of what we are thinking about other people we are in a relationship with. Empathy is necessary in order to sense the other's circumstances and learn from what their experiences have taught them. Without empathy, there is not deep connection with the other person. We need to share with them genuinely.

You need to use your ability to feel empathy for others in order to look at a situation from another person's perspective, which you'll soon learn is one of the reframing methods. By using empathy, you will learn what plausible understandings there might be to explain why the other person's actions or behaviors are creating stress in you. When we understand, we can move forward.

Empathy requires that the adult Self take the lead and help you navigate the other person's behavior or words. If you stay in your hurt child Part, that child Part will block your ability to perceive an explanation and understanding of what is driving the other person, causing them to say something or behave in a non-adult manner.

Empathy toward Self and others helps to set the stage for forgiveness, which is necessary in order to get unstuck from a hurtful place and to manage anxiety.

> *People will forget what you said, people will forget what you did, but people will never forget how you made them feel.*
>
> —Maya Angelou—

SAMPLE REFRAMING 1

My mother always treats me as if I am a child. I am 28 years old and she still thinks that I am unable to manage my own eating habits.

See: the frustration and anger

Pheel: the irritation, lack of trust and respect.

Assess the intensity: 7

Positive statements:

> ➢ I am glad to know she continues to love me and care about me
>
> ➢ Without her care and attention over the years, I would have been at a loss
>
> ➢ I am thankful for my mother and forgive her for her worries
>
> ➢ I am a fully functional adult
>
> ➢ I am capable of making healthy food choices
>
> ➢ She just needs to be my friend
>
> ➢ I want her to trust me

Alternate thought: *I really appreciate your concern for my health and nutrition. I have always felt your love and support. I would like it if our relationship could shift from being a parent/child relationship to being more like a friendship where we give each other mutual respect.*

I promise you that I will be responsible for my health and make healthy food choices but those choices may not always line up with yours because I have different needs from you. Please trust me and be my dearest friend.

SAMPLE REFRAMING 2

You are feeling very depressed and anxious about the lack of time you have had to spend with your spouse lately. They keep so busy that communication between the two of you has really fallen off. You feel abandoned. It seems as if your spouse is always making something else a higher priority than you. You tolerate the disconnection to keep the peace.

What does tolerance accomplish?

Tolerance, in this situation, is a type of avoidance—avoidance is toxic to relationships. Avoidance means you are choosing not to join in union toward the original shared goal of living together in harmony and love. You are struggling with whether or not to speak up and talk together about what you are feeling.

By not talking together, you are avoiding. Avoidance means you are choosing to *tolerate* the abandonment. This choice will not lead to resolution, and this choice comes from your hurt child Part. Avoidance is not an adult decision or choice.

Choosing to avoid a confrontation will prevent you from learning what your reality is. Avoidance will not allow you to learn what benefit could result from taking a risk. Choosing to face a situation, and creating a new experience through risk-taking is how we learn and grow.

In order to evolve—we must continue to collect new knowledge. Knowledge is gained through experience. You have at your fingertips the potential to create a learning laboratory on life through planned risk taking.

Sometimes couples living together believe keeping the peace is a sign of a good healthy relationship. They believe that disagreement might reflect turmoil, failure in the relationship, or dissatisfaction between partners. THE REVERSE IS TRUE.

A healthy relationship model exists when partners can come from different perspectives, share, hear, and understand each other's viewpoints, find their common goals and compromise until both partners walk away feeling heard, understood, and both of them feeling satisfied with the resolution. There must be give and take in compromise.

A mutually satisfactory resolution reflects a healthy relationship whether it is between friends or partners. It is not realistic to think that living in harmony does not include negotiation and that sometimes the negotiation requires taking it in steps or with breaks but always returning to the negotiation table, so to speak, until satisfactory resolution has been achieved. Accomplishing resolution together will fill each partner with a strong connection to the other, a sense of shared fairness and commitment, and it will fill their home with peace.

RETURNING to the reframing example, you find yourself ruminating over your feelings of rejection, sadness, fear for the future and how little time you have with your spouse. The mental chatter and sleeplessness are beginning to fill your mind and keep you awake, either when trying to fall asleep or from falling back to sleep when you wake during the night.

There have been two or three nights each week of significant sleep loss, and that is making it more difficult to get through your days. You are feeling tired and depressed (choosing to be depressed rather than choosing to take action).

Your avoidance in talking to your spouse happens to be familiar to you and, therefore, it is comfortable. It is the usual tactic you use to handle difficult situations. Avoidance will lock-up your feelings and inhibit movement. Avoidance leads to your relinquishing your value.

Remember how we identified depression as a tendency to spiral down. Avoidance will not provide you with any new information or any opportunity to talk or take action to work through a problem to bring resolution. Avoidance will not attend to your desires and needs to create any upward movement in spirit. Avoidance will perpetuate your downward spiral.

What can you choose to do?

Let's go to the SPA

S — See the anxiety

P — Pheel the feeling

A — Alternate thought to be substituted

See what you are feeling and hearing — confused voices, feeling a lack of sleep, and feeling anxious, sad, and rejected.

Pheel the rejection your spouse is projecting. They are choosing to spend their time elsewhere or in some other activity that excludes you. Where do you fit into their priority lineup? How does that make you feel?

Assess your intensity: 10+

Accept that it is rejection that you are experiencing. Spend some time with that feeling of rejection because this is probably not the first experience you have had with it. Either your spouse has elicited those feelings in you in the past and/or it may be going back further in your development to a significant person or friend from your past.

How does the sadness feel in your heart? You learn who you are by traveling your heart's history. The intensity of the feelings that are surfacing now, demonstrates the past effort and strength it must have required for you initially to pull through those difficult times.

It is not helpful to criticize yourself for having these feelings. They are legitimate feelings that any human being would experience under similar circumstances. This is how we learn about ourselves—by creating a re-enactment of our history and learning what we had to do to survive. You will discover how exceptionally smart and brave you were.

Today, you have been working with yourself and connecting to your heart and you understand how negative energy needs to be transformed into positive energy in order to move through your anxieties.

Assess your intensity: 10 (This is a tiny reduction. You are beginning to recognize your needs and we are stirring up strong feelings. You are still in a decision-making stage and very apprehensive, so your intensity remains high.)

After spending time learning about why you are sensitive to rejection—the next step is to lead yourself using adult thinking and decision making. Leading yourself through **self-parenting** is what starts to change your neural pathways and starts the process of permanent change in how you think and function in navigating life.

Take your cleansing breath combined with your visual image and stay with those for a minute or two. Remembering the strategies of forgiveness and empathy in approaching this situation, use your adult Self to find forgiveness in your heart and empathy for what your partner may be dealing with.

Alternate thoughts to be substituted: **I choose to oppose this feeling of rejection** or **I choose to question this feeling of rejection and learn the truth.**

Consider how it would feel if you substituted the words "choose to oppose" the rejection rather than "tolerate" the abandonment. "Abandon" is a verb that another person "chooses to co" to someone. To abandon gives all the action and power to the abandoner, thus leaving you, the abandoned one, in the powerless position of victim.

To "oppose" the rejection is a verb that calls you to action in response to the other person's behavior. It can be empowering, yet it might also be terrifying.

If we do not like how we are being treated, we must change something in *our* behavior that will cause them to respond to us differently. Give up the tolerance and avoidance—employ discussion and compromise with empathy.

If you were to approach your spouse and verbally oppose or question the rejection you have been feeling, I suspect it would feel very risky. It would probably skyrocket your anxiety because your habit has been avoidance.

The thought of stepping out of your familiar habit of avoidance will likely be terrifying. It would be putting peace at risk. It might expose you to your spouse's anger, further rejection, or even punishment by your spouse.

Courage doesn't mean you don't get afraid. Courage means you don't let fear stop you.

—Bethany Hamilton—

Which is worse—continuing on with anxiety, feeling rejected, and struggling with sleeplessness, or hearing the truth about their feelings or thoughts? You may not like hearing the truth, but avoiding it will keep you stuck in your worst fears. There may be things your spouse has been dealing with from work and all the chores have been his distraction. His busyness may have nothing to do with his feelings toward you.

If you learn the truth, it will provide you with information. Information takes you out of the dark. Revealing your feelings of rejection might wake your spouse up to empathize with what you have been experiencing. Discussion and compromise will involve dialogue, time together, and sharing.

The information you gain through communication will lead to choices you can make based on their response and give you some control over your future. Choosing to repeat the familiar, comfortable method of acceptance by silence devalues you, your needs, and your desires that comprise your "quality world" (Glasser, 1999). You are entitled to this information.

Who do you need to have at your side to navigate this oppositional position? Would your adult Self be capable of handling this opposition—certainly more so than your fearful rejected Part.

This is an opportunity to stretch outside of your comfort zone and take a risk. If you decide to choose to oppose your spouse's behavior, what happens to your depression? Do you feel some energy stirring within? Depression saps us of energy. Harness your energy and use it to create change.

Problems are only opportunities in work clothes.

—Henry J. Kaiser—

Calling forth your adult Self to forgive and find empathy for your partner and choosing to take an action with self-leadership can generate a new sense of energy and direction that will lead you away from depression.

Right now, you simply need to decide if you will choose to take action. You can work on how to make the approach shortly and I will help lead you through that step.

Repeat your **alternate thoughts**: *"choose to oppose"* or *"choose to question and learn"* and determine the level of your anxiety and sadness on the intensity scale after substituting those words.

Assess your intensity: it is a 9+ (You have decided to take an action and that brings forth some positive energy but you still have to determine how to move forward—the intensity will lessen as you make your plan and it will be further alleviated after you have taken the action).

This may still feel very risky, even scary, because it is a new approach to how you have handled problems in the past. Opposing their rejection might be a difficult choice. You may be afraid of your spouse's response.

Next step—make a physical list of what points you want to say to your spouse. The anxiety-lowering decision here is that you have decided not to remain silent any longer. You have "chosen to speak" and use your voice. The fact that you have made that decision will relieve some amount of angst. Taking action gives you a sense of control.

Assess your intensity: 9

The problem of how you can present this talk to your spouse is scary. Take several cleansing breaths, use your visual imagery, and stay with the relaxed feeling that it induces for a few minutes. It will help to energize you for this next step. Stop reading and take the next few minutes to think of positive statements you could say to your spouse that demonstrate your caring and appreciation for them.

Sample Approach: considering your spouse may not be a person who is open to challenges about their behavior, how would it seem to you to think about making *statements* about what is positive followed by a *question* about the situation?

Some Positive Statements Might Be

> ➢ I know you enjoy all your activities around the house.
> ➢ I love to see you happy and productive in doing the things you love.
> ➢ I know that it is important to you to keep up with the work and not fall behind.
> ➢ I get the benefit of seeing things around the house and yard look nice.
> ➢ I thank you for all you do in keeping everything looking so nice.
> ➢ When you get free time after your chores, I am happy to see you spend time with your friends, golfing or socializing, because I know you enjoy that, it gives you a break and you deserve that.

Here are some sample statements followed by a thoughtful question

Combine two of the positive statements above, followed with your thoughtful questions.

> ➢ Thank you for all the work you do around our home. When you keep busy with activities throughout the day, we do not get much time together. Do you notice that?

➢ You keep our home looking so nice. I appreciate how much time that takes out of your day. I miss our time together. How about you? Is there a way we could set aside regular together time?

➢ Sometimes, I wonder if you are tending to avoid time with me—am I wrong in my thinking?

An Example: *I know that it is important to you to keep up with the work around the house, and that after getting home from work or on the weekend after doing those chores, you do not have much spare time for yourself. We do not get much time together either and I miss that. How about you? Is there a way we could set aside some regular together time?*

Write out the words that fit well and resonate with you

This approach speaks to your spouse as an adult partner, and you are running the house together. It complements them and thanks them for their time, energy, skills, and talents. This approach should elicit their adult Self to respond because they will hear appreciation, not criticism, which should open their heart to honestly hearing you and your words of concern. It is likely to elicit their empathy and therefore, a connection between both of your hearts.

If you speak to their adult Part with fairness and without criticism and guilt, more than likely they will respond in kind.

Assess your intensity: it is down to a 7 (you can begin to see a pathway)

That is a significant reduction in your anxiety level. The final reduction will result when you have taken the action/risk and voiced your fears, so you can hear their reality.

Chances are your partner will respond in a similar tone and want to attend to your needs as well as theirs. Whatever the outcome, you have chosen an action—that is positive and you will gain information from that action in how to move forward. You will have experienced replacing the apprehension with positive action to gain helpful information. This is huge—congratulations!

If your partner's response does not lead to resolution, then use similar steps to work through what needs to be the next exchange between you. Step away and recover from your risk-taking. When you feel ready again, you can begin to plan the next discussion.

Do not give up and go back to avoidance. You are poised for action—maintain that posture—you need to understand what is happening between you both so you can sleep again. Not understanding what is going on will only perpetuate more stress, harm to your health, days filled with turmoil, and an inequity in your home.

Assess your intensity: 5-6 (now it is time to follow through)

These are life-changing strategies that will serve you well for the rest of your life and open up the possibility for deeper relationships with everyone you know. Your friends and family will see a new you.

Chapter Wrap-up

Up to this point, we have covered a great deal of background information, interesting theories, and the building-block strategies of mindfulness, visual imagery, self-awareness, insightfulness—and from this chapter—forgiveness, and empathy. With these building-block strategies, your comprehensive plan is taking shape.

You have been stepping through clearing your mind and relaxing your body in response to the self-awareness of stress rising within you. You are gaining insights and learning to identify emotions that need healing within you. You are ready to face your fears. You are learning that forgiveness and empathy expressed towards others and to yourself will greatly support you in your effort to reduce the anxiety, stress, and tension that you often experience.

If we could look into each other's hearts and understand the unique challenges each of us faces, I think we would treat each other much more gently, with more love, patience, tolerance, and care.

—Marvin J. Ashton—

Your Action Plan

> By now, you are getting more comfortable with the basic strategies so that overlaying the forgiveness and empathy strategies will provide deeper connection to yourself as well as others. Your comprehensive plan is gaining depth and dimension.

> Taking as many opportunities to implement these various behavioral strategies as often as possible will continue to build your self-knowledge so that you are even more successful with the reframing techniques we are headed to and will learn about in chapter 10.

> Together, I can help you connect to your heart.

Chapter 9 presents the significant strategies of creating new habits (strategy 7) and risk-taking (strategy 8), which will lead to growth-producing results. You are ready for these strategies and action.

Reframing—How Do You Get Some?

*The reality of life is that your
perceptions—right or wrong—
influence everything else
you do. When you get a proper
perspective on your perceptions,
you may be surprised how many
other things fall into place.*

—Roger Birkman—

Chapter 9 challenges you to commit to bringing change into your life through habit formation and risk-taking, the seventh and eighth of our building-block strategies. It will be your dedication to those objectives that will lead to your success with reframing—supporting your growth and your greater goal of peace. Strategies seven and eight will solidify your reframing technique.

STRATEGY 7—CREATE NEW HABITS

The generally accepted time it takes to create a new habit is approximately three weeks. However, during that three-week period, you must practice the habit regularly, consistently, and without deviation. Establishing the habit of any of the building-block strategies as well as the habit of the reframing technique requires patience, discipline, commitment, and frequent time slots carved out of your day so that you get the needed practice.

You can approach the practice as a challenge to yourself—something to be excited about because it will bring you more control over your whirling thoughts. Awareness of your whirling thoughts gives you the opportunity to cognitively choose to replace them with one of the other strategies you have been practicing and that will build toward making it a habit.

There is no failing because every time you take an opportunity to practice any of the given strategies, it will make the next effort easier and more automatic.

Strategies 7 and 8 are the strategies that truly start to transform your life. You have been digesting a ton on information and you are now posed to take on the last step in this learning process. I am so proud of your diligence and commitment.

Adding humor and the ability to recognize baby-step progress will help to make it more fun and having fun with it will increase your commitment and success. Please celebrate your baby steps as you work with strategy 7 and 8 because this is where you will truly start to grow. The baby steps are really very significant strides. Small wins are big wins!

However far you propel yourself along this journey, you will gain a deeper understanding of yourself and others. With every step toward self-understanding and self-acceptance you make, you will attain a greater degree of comfort in life.

I achieved the benefits and skills from the 8 strategies and reframing by using them regularly, which proved the reliability of the all of it. I continually defined which Part of me was in charge, and used non-stop, objective self-awareness. I understood I *needed* to make changes so with persistence, insightfulness, and patience, I became committed to the end result I wanted.

My goal was to prove to myself that life did not have to be so intimidating. Using daily situations to create a laboratory on life allowed me to replace and discard the old beliefs that were crippling me—and to instill reframing along with the building-block strategies as habits in my life. Over time, I developed efficiency and efficacy through daily practice—and daily practice over time will lead to your neurological changes—you can expect the same.

Motivation is what gets you started. Habit is what keeps you going.

—Jim Ryun—

If you study and implement some level of reframing along with the building-block strategies or only get as far as practicing mindfulness and then have to set the work aside for a time, you will not lose much ground. You can return to the practices when the time is right again for you. This is a building process, so any effort you put forth today will contribute to your ultimate goal.

Every step will add foundation to the skills you learn and practice. Collectively, every effort, energy and step you direct toward your ultimate goal will take you closer to the peace you are seeking. Opening this book has been the beginning of your journey—choose to discover where you will lead yourself.

Thich Nhat Hanh describes, "habit energy" as the energy we spend throughout the day performing daily habitual routines or simple tasks http://www.ancientbrain.net/home/ancient-brain/thich-nhat-hanh-habit-energy/. Some of those routines might look like brushing teeth, washing the dishes, walking the dog, or taking out the garbage.

He describes habit energy or "habit behavior" as repeating patterns of mindless behavior—doing and thinking things throughout the day without thought. It is a strong energy, meaning you do not forget to do it, because it is so practiced.

You need to develop that strong "habit energy" around reframing and the accompanying building-block strategies.

Neuroscientists have determined that habit-making behaviors are established in the area of the brain called the basal ganglia where emotion, memories and patterns are developed whereas—in-the-moment decisions are made in the prefrontal cortex.

Scientists have found that habits are simple brain cell connections that lead to "habit behavior" and that they can be replaced by mindfully becoming aware of the habit and actively establishing a healthier habit to replace it. Thich Nhat Hanh wants us to become mindful of our old "habit behavior" or "habit energy," overcome it and replace it.

According to neural expert, Dr. Joe Dispenza in Ted Talk—Tacoma, repeating behaviors reinforce neural bonding. https://www.youtube.com/watch?v=ZjNSwUb_Sj4. In this 17 minute Ted Talk, he explains how you achieve new "habitual neural networking" through the consistent repetition of new behaviors.

By mindfully disconnecting the old habit wiring and establishing new neural bonds through repeated behaviors, a desired habit can be strengthened until it reaches the habit status. Dispenza recognizes that the old habit wiring in the brain is harder to "rewire" than newer habits but with time and persistence, it can and will be accomplished.

With "habit energy," the brain almost shuts down and the routines and behaviors are on automatic pilot. This is advantageous because it allows for multitasking; however, if those habit energies are detrimental, such as obsessive thinking, they can be destructive.

In general, if you tend to obsess and can't seem to stop or move through obsessive thinking, then a very effective **alternative thought** for any obsessive thinking is:

This is just an obsessive thought—that is my *reality* at this moment—if I do not allow my thoughts to continue or to effect my behavior, the thought will pass, it will go away and the obsessions will stop. I need to busy myself with another activity to focus my attention away from my obsessive thinking (Dr. Joe Brown).

Before you can insert this **alternate thought**, you must be aware of your obsessive chatter so that you can "choose to handle it."

Repeating this **alternate thought** to yourself while employing deep breathing to help you stay focused and in the present moment as you get involved in a new activity is how you can lead yourself through your obsessive thinking or behavior. Repeating this behavior can begin to establish new neural networking.

We are what we repeatedly do.
Excellence, then is not an act,
but a habit.

—Aristotle—

Thich Nhat Hanh instructs us to take that "habit energy" and transform it into mindfulness energy so that we can use it to live fully in every moment of our daily life with mindfulness of everything we do, think, and feel. Using mindfulness in everything you do will provide significant stress reduction in itself because when you are using mindfulness, you have cut out the extraneous chatter. Make mindfulness a new "habit behavior."

You will need to use your transformed "habit energy" in incorporating reframing and the accompanying building-block strategies as a viable resource in life. Habit energy will bring about your transformation.

STRATEGY 8—RISK-TAKING

Webster defines risk as "an exposure to a hazard or danger." What I want you to accept and believe is that risks do not always mean something is life-threatening or posing potential bodily harm. Instead, recognize that risk-taking may *feel* like a significant hazard or danger even though the actual danger may not be threatening to your safety.

Taking risks in life is always scary. It takes you out of your comfort zone and exposes you to possible rejection, judgment, failure, hurt, or pain—none of those are life threatening.

By risk-taking, I am asking you to consider stepping outside of your comfort zone to test the waters. I am suggesting that you begin taking a risk by doing or saying something that people have not heard or seen you do or say before.

It could be as simple as making eye contact with a person you pass on the street or in the elevator, and smiling at them. You might try talking to a stranger at the deli counter or in line at check out. Find something that feels uncomfortable— use it to create a potential risk-taking event. Taking risks is how your confidence will begin to develop.

Confidence grows from risk taking because through risk taking you learn to handle life, learn to address your needs, learn what you think and start believing in yourself. Confidence means you will no longer feel you need to qualify, apologize, or put yourself in second place. All of these entitlements are waiting for you on the other side of FEAR.

Deciding to take some risks, in and of itself, may feel very scary. What may be a risk to one person may not necessarily be a risk to another person. It will be very individualistic. The concept of taking risks means putting yourself out there in life and beginning to experiment in order to discover new possibilities for growth.

Risk-taking will provide you with new feedback. The new feedback will gradually begin to challenge your old beliefs and ways of coping. Your old beliefs are just strong habits and they *can* be replaced.

You have a choice. You bought this book because you were hoping there might be a way to learn to manage your runaway thoughts. You started this book with the purpose of making a change. Is there an obstacle in your path to making that change?

Time constraints and schedules can be worked around. Could it be fear based on old beliefs? Could it be habits you need to break? Could the safety measures of your comfort zone be keeping you from moving forward?

*Goals are like beacons
in the ocean that
guide the ship to safety.*

—Scott Allan—

Let's Reframe Risk-taking

When I suggest that you take risks, it would not surprise me that it may cause you to feel quite uncomfortable. Therefore, I want to spend some time looking at risk-taking from another perspective. We will reframe it.

I have tried to establish the idea that taking a risk has the potential to cause an individual to feel some level of discomfort, danger, or pending judgment. In a preceding paragraph, I suggested that saying hello to a stranger and making eye contact are forms of risk-taking for some individuals.

In reality, the so-called risk is certainly not a tremendous hazard or danger, yet it can feel something like that because

I am asking you to challenge your old beliefs and the rules you have lived by. They have been your comfort zone or habits for decades.

So here is your risk-taking reframed as you begin to feel fear rising at the *idea* of taking a risk:

> ➢ Hello fearful emotions;
>
> ➢ welcome your presence, and recognize you are my old FRIENDS making me aware of my fearful emotions;
>
> ➢ Thank you for showing yourself because it reminds me I have lots to gain by risk-taking practice —I need to harness my fears and choose to challenge them by risk-taking practice;
>
> ➢ t will provide me with OPPORTUNITIES to discover my strengths, transform my weaknesses into strengths, and recognize that my negative emotions are not based on reality.

Life opens up opportunities to you, and you either take them or you stay afraid of taking them.

—Jim Carrey—

The risk (feeling discomfort) now presents as an opportunity (chance to grow). It has been reframed. This reframing of your initial fearful reaction to the idea of taking a risk should somewhat help to offset the panic at the suggestion. The risk can now be seen as an opportunity to initiate the start of a *more comfortable* life rather than as a risk that might bring a judgment or negative consequence.

Risks are opportunities to turn your negative emotions into chances for growth and learning from the feedback obtained by taking the risky action. The feedback will be based on reality. As a matter of fact, it is your anxious feelings about taking the risks that are solely based on your old misperceptions, negative self-beliefs, or self-established personal rules. These are what have been imprisoning you—it is time to harness them and set yourself free.

Each reader will likely have different types of risks to experiment with and different types and levels of anxiety to overcome. Believe it or not—as time goes on with your risk-taking, it can become fun and exciting.

The physical symptoms of stress are your Parts sending you a warning, shouting at you to pay attention, and begging you to self-parent your way through the turmoil.

EXAMPLE 1 OF RISK-TAKING

Say you are a person with a fear of dogs. When you were a little child, a dog bit your nose, so the thought of going up to a dog could be very scary—even paralyzing.

Assess your intensity: 7–8

Alternate thought: I will substitute the words **opportunity for growth** whenever I formulate a plan to take a risk. In this case, it is in regards to my fear of dogs. Here is my risk.

I will make an *opportunity for growth* today by petting a dog in the park so that I can learn dogs can be friendly.

Assess your intensity: 6

Formulated Plan:

My "opportunity for growth" today will be to ask the owner of a dog in the park if I may slowly approach their dog. If the owner assures me that it is safe to do so, I will hold out my hand and slowly walk toward the dog and allow that dog to sniff my hand. The dog's reaction will provide me with a new experience that I can begin to collect toward offsetting my fear of dogs. If the dog is friendly, I will spend a few minutes petting it.

Assess your intensity*:* 4 (It will be further reduced after the risk has been executed.) Pride, excitement, relief and elation will be felt. This risk should be employed several more times on different occasions.

Repeating the executed risk will continue to reduce apprehensions incrementally with each subsequent experience. Before too long, you will smile when you encounter a safe dog (always check with the owner first to make sure the dog is friendly). Each risk will get a little bit easier to undertake than the one before. This is where you will grow confidence. Confidence is not something that magically appears one day—it has to be developed.

The amount of rejection, failure, pain, or hurt you may anticipate from taking a risk may feel absolutely paralyzing. In reality, if a planned risk is isolated and examined by itself, it can be evaluated and understood not to be a huge risk.

Take a moment to think of a simple action you might plan as a risk-taking experiment. Let's consider attending an exercise class or getting a massage (if you have never had a massage previously). Neither of these suggested activities is dangerous, but the potential level of discomfort to be experienced by putting yourself into one of those new circumstances might feel extremely threatening.

Explore these fears and determine what part of those new experiences is causing you unrest? Could it be the discomfort of people seeing you exercise or the idea of someone seeing or touching your body in the massage?

Break the risk down into baby steps—for example, just visit a facility to pick up a schedule. At the next visit, spend a little more time just being there or if you are really brave, talk with a staff member. Gradually build up your comfort level with each exposure.

The mere idea of planning a potential risk provides you with an example of just how anxiety-producing risk taking can make you feel. This in-the-moment fear at the prospect of taking a risk has stimulated a memory from within your amygdala, or has triggered one of your negative self-beliefs or old safety rules, causing your brain to send a message to your adrenal glands to release cortisol.

The cortisol triggers your muscle tension and apprehension sets in. In the present moment, you can feel the worry that the mere idea of taking a risk is causing within you. That is your muscle memory being recalled.

Taking risks and exposing yourself to the consequences of taking a risk needs to be initiated with tiny, baby-size risks and even taking baby steps that lead up to that first baby-size risk. No step can be too small.

At this point, the most important thing to understand is that everyone has some level of fear or discomfort at some points in their life. You are not alone. Everybody has inner fears to varying degrees. This is a worldwice club—welcome! Fear does not discriminate, and fear is an equal-opportunity reality.

Opportunities are like sunrises.
If you wait too long,
you miss them.

—William Arthur Ward—

EXAMPLE 2 OF RISK-TAKING

When I first began to understand that my freedom lay in relearning life, I understood that I needed to set up experiments to prove to myself that my old beliefs and fears were not founded on reality. I believed risk-taking was my key to freedom!

I made risk-taking a daily job to perform. My repetitive old negative self-beliefs had to be tested, retested and tested again. I tell you all this because I want to give you hope that change is possible.

Before I went to work each day, I had a plan for that day as to how I could test one of my core beliefs in my effort to relearn how to relate to people and prove to myself I would remain safe and learn to be more comfortable with taking risks.

I actively sought out practice times each day by placing myself into anxiety-causing situations to disprove my negative core beliefs. Creating these daily experiments would yield outcomes to demonstrate to myself that my fears were not reality-based—I have learned I am able to engage in life *despite* my fears. This approach will work for you. Six months from now, I predict you will wake up in the morning feeling more energized.

Start with very tiny risks that most other people would not consider a true risk but to you, are terribly threatening. Risk-taking is a powerful tool that yields positive results, it challenges your old beliefs, and allows you to see and live a new outcome. New outcomes build confidence.

Deposit the new outcomes into your bank account of positive results to gradually replace old beliefs and allow you to believe in the possibility of a new reality. Learning and beginning to believe in the possibility of a new reality will gradually lead to trust, confidence, and movement toward more comfort in life. Your new reality will set the stage for your growth.

For me, asking questions is paralyzing. I would plan a question to ask the office manager or one of the dentists. It did not matter what the question was. It could be a very simple request for some piece of information or it might be a request for some personal time off. I pledged to myself that I would ask that question before the end of the each day.

Trust me, it was always late afternoon before I was able to follow through. It took me the entire day to build up my courage to get to the point where I could take the risk to ask the simplest of questions. The anticipation of standing in front of an authority figure and asking my planned question in a clear audible voice felt debilitating, like I was putting myself at risk for some form of rejection.

I would have to work up my courage and talk myself into it for half the day. I promised myself I would not go home before I had performed my experiment. I always kept those promises to myself. You need to keep your promises to yourself, too. Your confidence and comfort level will increase.

As time went on and I experienced more positive outcomes than when I was a child, I increased the risk-taking to asking bigger questions or relating an anecdote at lunch with several co-workers sitting around the table. Previously, just opening my mouth to talk was terribly threatening.

When I think back to how painful that risk-taking was, I celebrate my bravery. I want you to know I understand fear. My point is—we have to be our own advocates and create the relearning experiences that provide us with opportunities for our personal growth. Others will not do that for us. And all of us have a need to grow personally.

To this day, I remain actively committed to looking for opportunities to take risks—I understand that I still need to continue to grow and not fall back into old habits. I continue to work on expanding my comfort level every day.

I have learned that regularly placing myself in challenging or uncomfortable situations, in order to disprove old negative beliefs, allows me to continue to gain positive feedback so that I reinforce my new ways of thinking and responding to life. I want to continue to move forward in my goal of being fully engaged in life.

I explain this here so that you can again grasp the concept that this truly is a life journey. Every step brings you closer to your goal, and deepens your commitment. Living freely will start to become your reality.

Life begins at the end of your comfort zone.

—Neale Donald Walsch—

Challenge and Growth

Where will risk-taking lead you? Exposing yourself to taking risks will provide you with experiences to measure against your old fears. Taking new risks and exposing your fears to the risk-taking process will provide you with new validating feedback that will yield the beginnings of change in you.

Taking risks will allow you to feel a magnification of those old fears that are now out of proportion to the present day risk-taking experiment. Planning the risk will evoke strong body sensations within you that demonstrate how easily those sensations are elicited under very normal, everyday situations.

You will see that the simple risk you want to attempt feels so much more difficult than it should actually be—proving everything we have been discussing. Taking risks and accumulating the positive results will hopefully motivate you to experiment more frequently and freely so that you can more quickly unshackle your life.

How would reliving an experienced childhood fear through risk-taking provide insight? When anticipating a planned risk, you will become aware of the fear that is being elicited when just *thinking* about the potential risk. You are only thinking about a potential situation, not living through the actual situation.

Assess your intensity. Does this not provide you with an understanding of the fear level you must have felt at one time? This is a significant insight.

It is my guess that many of you know exactly what I am talking about. I have had to ask myself, "How can the small simple act of asking a simple question put a tailspin on my day? What is going on? What is being triggered?"

The "yes" or "no" response to a simple question is not life threatening; it is not going to cost me my job, yet that is how frightening it can feel. Become the researcher or scientist into your past to help you understand the present so that you can change your future.

Does the level of fear generated in you by the simple planning of a risk give you an appreciation of what life must have been like for you? Does simply thinking about a planned risk and experiencing the amount of unrest that it causes in the present moment give you an appreciation of the inner strength and resilience you must have had growing up to survive similar stresses as a child?

These are the resources in you that I want you to become aware of so that you can call on them to start to create the change you are seeking. These are the resources that you will use to self-parent yourself. These resources are your strength.

I have never been able to connect a particular past event to why I fear asking questions, but I have reasoned, based on my insights as well as what resonates in my heart, that my accumulated past experience taught me that my questions were often met with a lack of interest, a negative response (maybe with anger), potential rejection, or they were seen as a burden.

That is probably all the explanation I will ever be able to assemble, but it is enough because—our feelings represent our truth.

> *Take risks, be bold, and let your genius convert your fear into power and brilliance.*
>
> —Robert T. Kiyosaki—

Leaving Your Comfort Zone

Through risk-taking, you will learn so much about yourself. Risk-taking will provide you with a new awareness of yourself and sensitivity to life that may not have been your previous experience. Your old habit was avoidance and that habit has prevented new experiences from being available to you. It is time for a change.

Make opportunities to create these lessons by staging small risk-taking experiments in order to gain insights as to who you are. This will allow you to grow and change in how you interact in life. Eventually, it can lead to your having more confidence in dealing with people in most situations because knowing your inner resources, strengths, history, and your ability to survive promotes confidence.

Our comfort zones are simply the familiar, safe habits and guidelines we have established to navigate our days. Understanding that our comfort zones are simple habits, reframes the power they hold over us. Like all habits, they can be changed.

This reframing of the concept of comfort zones will free you to move beyond what is a comfortable habit and open you to greater potential. Therefore, your comfort zone is a place you are now ready to leave behind.

You purchased this book because you had a *desire* to create change—therefore, you are ready. Leaving your comfort zone is what will lead to freedom of choice, self-understanding, adventure, and freedom. Use risk taking as your catalyst for change.

The way to develop self-confidence is to do the thing you fear and get a record of successful experiences behind you. Destiny is not a matter of chance; it is a matter of choice. It is not a thing to be waited for; it is a thing to be achieved.

—William Jennings Bryan—

Risk-taking is a form of exposure therapy. I use exposure therapy with dentally phobic patients (about 20% of the general population is dentally phobic to some degree). My main objective in working with these patients over time is to provide them with positive experiences in the dental office where they become comfortable and in control of the situation as much as possible.

Their new positive experiences will replace the old fearful ones. This is called exposure therapy, as defined by Dr. Bourne in his *Anxiety and Phobia Workbook*. Controlled fearful situations are presented to systemically and sequentially expose a person to the feared object or situation, thus providing a new safe experience. Risk-taking equates to exposure therapy.

With repeated, new positive experiences to replace the traumatic past dental experiences they suffered, these patients can gradually begin to trust and tolerate sitting in the dental chair. They will never be relaxed and eager to be there, but after a year or so of hygiene appointments every 3 to 4 months, they can arrive at the office with a smile on their face and without sweat on their brow. I see this transformation regularly.

It is this reconditioning that gradually gives them a new reference point from which to anticipate their appointments. Each positive subsequent visit continues to buildup their emotional bank account of positive experiences gradually diminishing the strength of their phobia. Reconditioning (exposure therapy) takes time, but it is what you can expect will occur with consistent and sustained risk-taking on your part.

Just recently, I had a patient tell me she no longer needs to bring in her headset and music in order to "make it through her appointment." I have been seeing her every three months for four years. Her ability to do this has come from the replacement of old experiences with new experiences and trust.

I want this same result for you. I want you to achieve the same success and manage your fears through the practice of exposure therapy—it will initiate changes in your perceptions that will allow you to build trust in yourself and add to your peace. This is waiting for you.

I say this with confidence because I have lived this reincarnation myself. I have come from being someone who could not even ask another person to provide me with a ride home or to inconvenience them in some small way to being able to identify the lunacy of that situation and recognize it for being a very reasonable expectation in a relationship between two people who live fairly close to each other.

Today, I am able to ask for a ride without fear in my heart. The worst that can happen is that the person will say, "No," and I will need to make another arrangement—my taking a follow-up *reality check* will assure me that their, "No," was not a personal affront to me—they had a legitimate reason for not being able to accommodate my need.

Be a person who chooses to use these life-changing strategies to gradually gain more control over your life. Be a person who decides you have put yourself in a subordinate position long enough and you want to create a different life for yourself. Be the kind of person who empowers yourself and begins to use these tools to carve a pathway to your confidence and personal growth.

> ## *Opportunities don't happen; you create them.*
>
> —Chris Grosser—

Looking for your "windows of opportunity" to practice what you are learning and being dedicated to this journey by willingly staying the course will determine how quickly you move through the learning process and establish the new habits. *It's All About The Windows* is a very short book I wrote about finding time to fit new goals into your busy schedules. It is available for free download at: https://www.CreatingChangeLifeCoaching.com

If you are hoping to create a happier life, then the reframing and risk-taking discussed above can help take you in that direction. The clarity reframing brings will affect how you interact with people. A clear, focused adult mind means that you are taking into consideration all aspects of a conflict.

RISK-TAKING—BACK DOOR APPROACH REFRAMING

As an example of risk-taking, I'm going to share how I chose to experience my cancer treatment. I purposefully took a risk about my *attitude* toward the treatment and this risk stretched my comfort zone.

However, because of how I reframed my expectations, the risk I took ended up increasing my feeling of control and optimism—which is exactly what I needed when navigating the cancer experience.

In this example of leaving my comfort zone, you'll encounter a particular variation of reframing, one that I have dubbed the "back-door approach" reframing technique. I will explain the back-door technique more thoroughly in the next chapter.

For now, simply take in the risk-taking and the way that reframing worked to alleviate major anxiety and stress through this difficult experience.

I was diagnosed with appendiceal cancer in October 2014. It came as a huge surprise because over the past twenty years my husband and I have been "health nuts."

We became more and more educated about the impact of the American diet on physical health, and we made huge lifestyle changes to reduce our possibilities for a diagnosis of elevated cholesterol, heart disease, cancer, and diabetes. We continuously adopted new strategies and practices from that time to the present day.

People do not have any control over the unknown or the future. Humans can control their choices or behavior in the present moment when they possess good self-awareness. Future moments evolve out of present moment choices.

Given the cancer diagnosis, I needed to examine my in-the-moment choices in how to approach the surgeries, any treatment I might have to face, and the unknown outcome of the disease. On top of those challenges, I also felt high anxiety due to my childhood hospital experience. Without a doubt the cancer journey was going to take me out of my comfort zone.

In order to get through the entire ordeal, I knew I needed to look ahead at how I wanted to end up feeling when all was said and done. That is why I turned to using the back-door approach to reframing because, as you'll learn in the next chapter, when you reframe using the back-door approach, you start by determining how you want to feel or how you want things to be at the end of the experience.

I determined that if I chose to put my focus on my *daily attitude*, meaning my present moment choices, rather than the disease itself, that my maintained attitude would lead me to the end result I was looking for. Furthermore, there is quite a bit of literature available on the impact of a positive attitude on healing.

I reasoned that if I could sustain positive in-the-moment attitudes and face my evolving emotions as they arose, without fear, but with openness to learning and growth (here's the risk-taking part), that that daily attitude or mindset would stabilize me and take me through all the treatments. Staying cognizant of my present moment choices, rather than the disease itself, would lead me to the end result I was looking for.

If I had decided to avoid being open to processing my emotions and attitudes as they arose in real time, initially it would have yielded a safe, protective barrier to the roller coaster of emotions I might experience. However, those latent emotions would eventually have to be dealt with and processed. They would have surfaced later as generalized anxiety.

The internal stress caused by blocking any in-the-moment feelings would have maintained a heightened anxiety level keeping me in the flight or freeze mode (circulating the adrenal hormones) and that would have interfered with my healing.

The fight, flight, or freeze mode perpetuates apprehension, which maintains a focus on anticipated fear. Anticipation perpetuates a focus on the unknown. They all perpetuate the image of the "ghost" and BLOCK reality—allowing *fear* to dominate and keep you in a child Part.

In the following situation, I offer a dental office example of *sustained apprehension* and how it can be managed through the simple and always available tool of deep mindful breathing. The mindfulness breathing helps to keep the patient focused on the here and now stopping their escalating apprehensions.

When my dental patients are tied up in the *anticipation* of pain, it blocks the reality of what is actually being felt. I may cause them a nanosecond of minor discomfort from touching an exposed root surface with an instrument; however, in their mind they begin to focus on the anticipation of sustained pain or an increasing level of pain.

They anticipate the "ghost," which is far worse than the reality of the moment. They tense up and stay tensed up because their fearful anticipation that I may touch another sensitive area or that the pain will increase in intensity is their expectation.

Their anticipation of pain is coming from a past dental office situation which did involve pain and where they did not feel they had any control. Fear and muscle tension dominated their entire experience. That fear became imprinted as a need to fear dentistry in general.

Even if no discomfort is experienced throughout their present-day office visit, their anticipation of expected pain along with the intense emotions sustained throughout the appointment keeps the patient in a heightened state of arousal. They bring that heightened state of arousal back with them to their next appointment because they left believing that pain was their reality.

Their reality is based on old emotional fears that will generate a high level of fearful apprehension when returning for their next visit. They hold a negative understanding of their present reality which perpetuates their past level of fear and anxiety and that creates a cycle of apprehension for every future appointment.

Their anticipation of expected dental office pain will keep them trapped in their state of overwhelming fear and apprehension. The goal is to bring them back to the present moment reality by having them center on their breathing.

I ask them to focus on their breathing and explain that any future discomfort will not increase in magnitude because I will not be doing anything different from what they have experienced thus far during the appointment. Talking about their fear demonstrates the value I give to their feelings.

I assure them that they have control and can say STOP and that I *will* stop. I continue to remind them to stay focused on the breathing, physiologically reducing the symptoms of anxiety and keeping them centered in the present moment reality.

By staying focused on their breathing and breaking the cycle of apprehension, they will leave with a different experience to reflect upon prior to their next appointment.

The same phenomena of anticipated fear would have pervaded my cancer experience. Not processing my emotions daily, while I was going through the trauma of the cancer, would have created the walled-off memories typical of PTSD. The walled-off memories would likely have created additional anxiety to have to be dealt with later. The memories would have been packed away during the height of my trauma and stored in the amygdala (the fearful memory storage file—chapter 3).

Later, when anxiety related to the cancer was triggered, the intensity of the anxiety would be equivalent to the original event, and I might not be able to connect those anxious feelings to the cancer but would simply feel terribly restless and apprehensive in general. You will recognize all of this discussion from chapters 2 and 3, but here I am using the cancer as another example of how anxiety can originate.

I could not control the disease, but I could have an impact on how I felt about it at the end of the treatments—coming out the back door. I determined that creating the end picture in my mind of how I wanted to feel at the end of each day would be my short-term focus.

So as not to burden my family with additional worry, I chose to cognitively process my apprehensions, keep positive, stay as active and self-sufficient as possible, and outwardly demonstrate an "I am OK" disposition as much as possible.

Sustaining that daily mindset yielded my desired long-term result.

I also "chose to experience" each day thoroughly rather than worry about the future prognosis. With this plan, I fully understood I would have to work at keeping in Self all the time.

I cannot always control
what goes on outside. But I can
always control what goes on inside.

—Wayne Dyer—

I did not want my family or me to be on a roller coaster ride dependent upon the ups and downs of every blood test result or CT scan, trying to determine what was happening on a daily basis. We needed to be patient and wait for the prognosis when procedures were done, treatment was finished, and the doctors had definite results that could be evaluated and measured.

I believed I needed to set the tone for how all of us would proceed through the year or two it would take until we had several screening tests following treatment.

Remember in chapters 1 and 7, where I said I understood one of my core beliefs was that I was responsible for everybody else's needs; well, here it is again—my feeling of needing to set the tone for everyone by stabilizing the roller coaster ride! The difference in this situation is I was conscious of that motivator yet I chose to take on that responsibility as a gift to my family. We have since passed that milestone, and I am in remission.

Taking a cleansing breath, using those objectives as my focus, and leading myself from an adult perspective, I chose to hold onto an "I can do this" attitude. The cancer had happened to us; there would be surgeries, tests, chemo treatment, sickness, recovery, healing, and strength building. We would handle all of that to some respectable degree along with support from family and friends.

All I needed to do was to SHOW UP so the medical staff could do their work. Paring away all the peripheral concerns I had no control over, cancer represented a big inconvenience with some personal discomfort. I did not want to fall back into living with generalized anxiety again.

I have had many dental patients who have gone through cancer diagnoses and treatment with many of them ending up suffering from extreme anxiety when they passed into their remission stage following their treatments. Those patients had not suffered from extreme anxiety prior to being diagnosed with cancer. Those patients had stuffed all their fears away to be dealt with after they were finished with treatment.

They chose not to face their fears as they arose, probably thinking that they just could not handle any more decisions or concerns at that time. Those patients chose avoidance. Avoidance created the "ghost" in their minds. I learned much from them, and I planned to use their experiences to my benefit.

By not facing and thinking about their anticipated or projected fears as they arose, they ended up experiencing greater anxiety after the fact. During their treatments most of their fears were about an unknown future, not about what was actually happening during treatment. In general, fears hold more power over people than reality—keeping us fearing the ghost created in our mind's painting.

Coming in through the back door, so to speak, gave me confidence because I could visualize where I wanted to end up and I knew I could accomplishment that by maintaining the leadership role over all my Parts. I needed to stay in Self.

I woke up every day appreciating the lessons in life I believed I was being given. In many ways, cancer can be a gift. A cancer diagnosis causes a reprioritizing of what is important, what quality of life is important to you for your remaining years, and the understanding and acceptance of life being finite.

Because I was not adjusting my fear reference point from day to day, I had peace. My reference point was a positive outcome far down the road—I did not vary that reference point. If I had focused on each step and what it might mean, I would have given away control of my thoughts and that would have kept me in a heightened state of arousal.

When necessary, I spent time allowing myself to feel poorly when I was discouraged or in pain. I faced my fears as they arose. I did not push them away or chastise myself for being human. I also used the two-week hospital stay to allow myself to feel the loneliness I must have experienced 63 years earlier from having been left alone in the hospital as an infant. The cancer experience provided me with many risk-taking opportunities and my confidence continued to develop.

During this hospital stay, I could soothe myself as an adult. The cancer center was 90 minutes from home, and my husband was very attentive, coming for long visits every other day over that two-week period, so I was not alone for the entire two weeks.

Nevertheless, sometimes I felt very lonely and very much a victim, but I did not chastise my husband. I also did not criticize myself for having selfish feelings nor did I try to avoid the loneliness. I used those feeling to help understand my original trauma.

Using the back door approach, my path became clear. I looked at how I wanted to end up feeling and thinking when all was said and done—working backwards to determine how to achieve my goal. I led myself through the mental planning and organization I needed to reach my desired outcome very quickly and with confidence.

By practicing reframing regularly in conjunction with the 8 building-block strategies, you too will be able to determine "solutions" quickly when major or minor anxiety suggests its presence in your life.

As long as you keep
on walking on the old paths,
you will never leave
footprints on the new paths!

—Mehmet Murat Ildan—

Chapter Wrap-up

> ➢ You have been encouraged to take the challenge to establish new habits, strategy 7, to alter or significantly change your life, as you have known it.

> ➢ You can create your own laboratory on life by experimenting with risk-taking opportunities, strategy 8, that will lead to personal growth.

> ➢ We have talked about the importance of leaving your comfort zone and designing your own "exposure therapy," so to speak. You read about my daily routine of purposefully leaving my comfort zone. Additionally you read about how new experiences provide relief to dental patients.

> ➢ Now the ball is in your court. Start with a tiny risk and build from there. Will you take it and run with it? Remember—your comfort zones are your habits, they can be changed and that happens with consistent baby steps!

> ➢ You do not have to do it alone. Together we could work through this process more quickly. Virginia@ CreatingChangeLifeCoaching.com.

Life is not about waiting for the storm to pass: it's about learning to dance in the rain.

—Unknown—

Your Action Plan

➤ It's time to practice strategies 7 and 8. While continuing to work on the habits of mindfulness/deep breathing, self-awareness, and visual imagery throughout your days, incorporate risk-taking opportunities regularly to promote your personal growth.

➤ Look for your opportunities to insert practice into your days. If you have not already downloaded my free book *It's All About the Windows*, it jumpstarts your creativity in finding timeslots in your day for creating change: http://www.CreatingChangeLifeCoaching.com

➤ Start putting small risk-taking experiments into every day—SET A POLICY—No day is complete until you have executed some small risk-taking effort. Make it your top priority! This would yield intentional risk-taking—doing it despite being scared and doing it because you are scared. Learn there is more to life than living in fear.

➤ Listen to this 17 minute Dr. Joe Dispenza TED Talk—Tacoma https://www.youtube.com/watch?v=ZjNSwUb_Sj4

➤ Consider scheduling an appointment with me from my website to initiate your transformation.

Chapter 10 provides the nitty-gritty of reframing with detailed descriptions of reframing variations that have evolved for me over the past 20 years as well as samples of each variation.

The Nitty-Gritty of Reframing Techniques

*Life is way too short to spend another
day at war with yourself.*

—Rae Smith—

Now that you've firmly established yourself in the 8 building-block strategies that assemble the foundation for your reframing practice, you are prepared to dive into reframing and its variations. And that's what this chapter provides—a presentation of each of the 7 variations of reframing that I have crafted, explained in careful steps, and supplemented with examples and suggested practices.

In chapter 10, you will note some repetition of material that was presented in earlier chapters in order to provide you with a cursory understanding of the reframing process to set the stage for some sample reframing examples. But the purpose of chapter 10 is to give you a full description of this powerful tool.

Therefore, I lay everything out for you in one chapter, which means there will be some redundancy. Perhaps, some of you have skipped the rest of the book and want only to focus on chapter 10—if that is the case, I would want you to have as much material as possible. Also, if you ever were to want to refer back to the reframing technique information in the future, having all aspects of the technique in one location in this learning guide would have great value.

As described in the beginning of this book, reframing takes a situation that is causing you anxiety and unrest, and within a couple of minutes turns your entire perspective around on the situation from being one of irritation, worry, or doubt—into one of calm, clarity, and confidence.

How can that happen in just a few short minutes? How can you transform those negative feelings just like that? When you are feeling turmoil, you are not able to view a situation from reality and from an adult perspective. You need to change that viewpoint—and that's what reframing allows.

Reframing entails your selecting the words that represent reality, quiets your fears, and provides hope. In reframing, you look at the situation, examine the feelings it has evoked in you from an adult perspective, and decide on an action or exchange the hurtful or fearful thoughts for words based on reality. The result is lowered anxiety.

Reframing will transform your stress, tension, and anxiety into confidence and peace. The following diagram illustrates the transformation of stress into confidence via reframing.

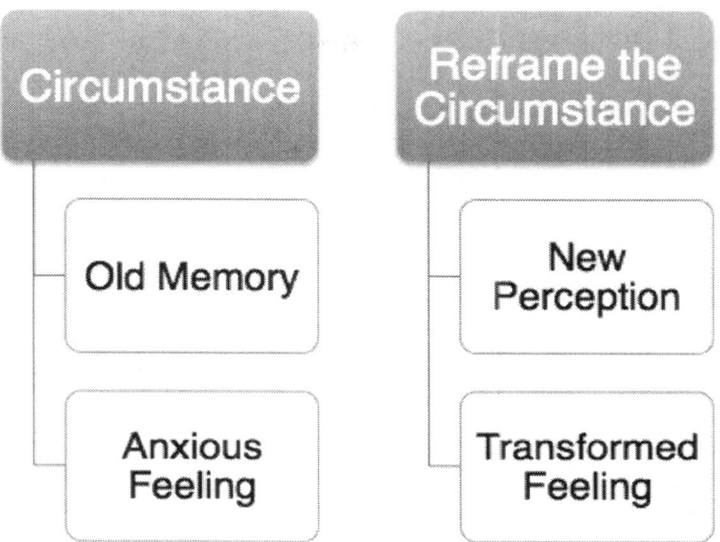

The trick in reframing is to recognize when your feelings are in need of attention. And that's why the building-block practices of mindfulness and self-awareness are key. Once you recognize the stress feelings coming on, identify which feeling is being triggered, you can then set the reframing in motion by selecting an **alternate thought** that will impact your worry and transform it into calm and confidence.

The intensity of the emotion should be immediately lessened by some measurable degree. If a further reduction in anxiety is needed, you can revisit the word or thoughts to select another thought that may resonate more fully.

Or take another minute to feel if there is an additional (hidden) emotion being elicited that also needs to have an **alternate thought** created to calm a below-the-surface triggered emotion.

In every situation and with every variation of the reframing technique, your *awareness* of an anxious feeling needs to initiate your first cleansing breath. As explained in chapter 5, that cleansing breath will trigger tension and stress reduction physiologically.

Success in reestablishing a calm state cannot be successful without your body being brought back into physiological balance first. Simultaneously bring forward your adult Self— requiring your Self to lead and parent.

Who Needs to Be Present to Reframe Successfully?

The temptation to stay in your child Part (chapter 5) will push strongly against your adult Self, trying to keep the adult Self from coming forward. Why?

In extremely simple terms, when we are afraid, hurt, or angry, we are hooked into strong child-like emotions. Your child Part is crying out to be nurtured, held, and comforted. We are going to nurture with reframing BUT not by reinforcing the helplessness.

Those hurt or angry feelings are familiar, like the proverbial "pair of old shoes." Because they are familiar, you accept them—you are used to wearing those feelings. The child-like reaction is one of your Parts playing out old dominant themes and beliefs that are familiar, and therefore comfortable. Decide it is time to rewrite the old patterns.

Your adult Self (chapter 4) can hold your child's hand. You can examine each situation that is causing the fear and select an **alternate thought** to use in each particular situation. Substituting a thought based on reality, rather than assumptions or fears, will empower you with positive energy.

The positive energy derived from the **alternate thought** will demonstrate the power of words. Allowing the anxiety to continue only perpetuates a physiological imbalance. Look beyond the tension, and trust your Self to lead you in "choosing to select" another thought—an adult thought that honors your fears and wants to calm them.

When you step up to the plate in your adult role, you are capable of providing another way to look at the stressful situation. In your mindful, adult state, you can employ forgiveness and empathy in viewing the other person's feelings and needs. Then exchange your present thoughts for a perspective that will allow you to view the situation and emotions objectively (hence, from a holistic perspective).

Telling yourself to "get over it" (which has a scolding tone) and to change your perspective does not usually work well, especially when fears or anger are dominant. You have to substitute the adult words, the **alternate thought**, from a parenting Self. The **alternate thought** must talk to your heart, which is how you always would have wanted your parents to speak to you.

By simply using neutral words to diffuse your emotions, you can calm yourself and trust the new words you choose to better represent the circumstances as they truly are, in reality. The new words will resonate with you as truth, which is what will allow you to feel calm and confident going forward. The transformed perspective will feel correct to you because it will resonate with your heart.

From this description you can see now how all the mindfulness and self-awareness practice you learned about in the initial chapters leads to insightfulness allowing you to eventually reframe simply and quickly. You have used mindfulness to bring yourself to the awareness of your feelings. It is those feelings that are causing you the unrest, and it is those feelings you want your **alternate thought** to impact.

He who knows others is wise.
He who knows himself
is enlightened.

—Lao Tzu—

A COLLECTION OF TECHNIQUES

There are several methods for reframing situations in our lives. Keep in mind that one variation may work better for you than another. Not every tension will be calmed in exactly the same way. One situation may reframe more successfully using one particular variation versus another. You may create your own personal preference or variation of the reframing tool.

I will review the different variations of reframing, including the SPA method, which has been explained and used in several examples throughout the book. As you will see, I also combine some of the techniques. Have fun with experimentation. These will be your reframing habits, so establish what works best for you.

No matter the reframing variation you work with, the common characteristics for resolving stress-inducing situations include: empathy for the other person's perspective, feelings, and needs; fairness in treatment to yourself as well as the other(s) involved; forgiveness to everyone involved; equitable treatment; honesty; a clear voice; self-leadership; and keeping a spiritual perspective.

The circumstances in which you can use reframing in your life are truly endless. I have come up with modifications to the SPA technique in order to fit it to different circumstances or to use a more expedient version to save time as I became more proficient with the skills. I did not find it beneficial to confine myself to a single basic template. I found I needed more flexibility.

These are the 7 reframing variations that we will explore:

- ➢ The "Going to the SPA" Reframing Technique
- ➢ Reframing Through Forgiveness
- ➢ Asking the "What If . . . Question" Reframing Method
- ➢ Back-door Approach Reframing
- ➢ Understanding Both Perspectives Reframing

> Reality-check Reframing Method

> Giving It to God Reframing—A Variation for Faith-based Readers

I strongly recommend you begin by using the SPA reframing technique and stay with it for a while to keep everything consistent and simple, learn where to insert it, recognize your feelings, and become efficient at creating **alternate thoughts**.

Initially, simply experience the benefit of reframing. The SPA technique provides a simple foundation for success and the SPA technique tends to be hurricane proof. I have crafted a refillable SPA practice template for you to download: http://bit.ly/ReframeSPA

THE SPA REFRAMING TECHNIQUE

"Going to the SPA" means that you go to a mentally-calming place that will revive your calm and restore stability to your day. The SPA reframing technique is excellent to use when starting out in actual real-life situations where you want to restore calmness. It has five simple steps that can be achieved relatively quickly and easily.

1. **See** what you are feeling.

2. **Pheel** and spend time with the emotion identified. Sort through the words (mental chatter) and circumstances, and give your heart time to identify and feel what you are feeling.

3. **Assess** the intensity of what you see and feel.

4. Substitute an **alternate thought**.

5. **Assess** the intensity after substituting the **alternate thought**.

*Great things are done
by a series of small things
brought together.*

—Vincent Van Gogh—

When you feel anxiety and mental chatter filling your head, right away that should send you a message of awareness that something in the situation is causing your strong reaction. You have to **STOP** and name what is going on: one or more of your child-like Parts is stepping up to bat at home plate. Out-of-bound reactions indicate an old wound is being triggered. Triggered emotions bring out the child in all of us.

In order to get your reactions under control, begin with your cleansing breath (described and explained in chapter 5) and take several breaths while using visual imagery (chapter 5) to help reverse the anxious physiological effects initiated by your hormones.

Then ask your adult Self to step up to the plate and take over. Ask your child Part to temporarily please sit on the bench. Only then will you be able to work through the situation, using the five steps, to bring resolution and calm.

Step 1: See

The S in SPA represents what you must **See**. You must *see* the anger, fear, hurt, sadness, or whatever feeling you are experiencing and is causing your anxiety and mental chatter. Seeing it will help you to identify it.

You need to see what you are feeling so that you do not avoid the fear, sadness, or other feeling. Whatever you are feeling is very important because it is a window into your hurt and what you feel is very important. Visualizing what you are experiencing creates a mental picture of your emotional state. You need to keep the visual part of your brain connected to the feeling part of your brain so that the situation can be properly processed and resolved.

Seeing causes you to become aware of the anxiety being triggered from a circumstance and notice how that affects you. Observe how fast your heart is beating. Is there a color associated with the feeling? I want you to visualize how the anxiety affects you—observe your posture, energy level, and attitude.

Step outside of yourself and observe your expression, the stress in your body, the muscle tension in parts of your body, such as in your face, shoulders, or stomach. Where do you feel the tension? I want you to identify what you **See** and acknowledge the reality of what you **See**.

Your moments of anxiety are mini-replicas of past situations, and your brain will want to disconnect its feelings from its cognitive processing to protect you from that original experience. Try hard to stay connected. Thorough resolution of anxiety requires that both the verbal and emotional components of the brain are working together and are connected to process the experience.

Step 2: Pheel

The P in SPA represents the **Pheelings** (feelings) the situation evokes. Identify what it is that you are *pheeling* and pair your feelings to what you are seeing. Name the feeling that you identify. Allow yourself time to experience the sensations of what it feels like to be angry, frustrated, rejected, hurt, etc.

Again, this requires establishing self-awareness and making a connection to your Self. Connecting to your heart will connect you to Self. Self-awareness puts you in touch with your soul. You cannot know who you are until you have explored your thinking and feeling processes.

The wisdom of your heart
is the connection to your
authentic power—the true
home of your spirit.

—Angie Karan—

Taking time with what you are feeling may be the first time in your life you have really connected with a feeling. Do not be afraid to feel it. It will not harm you although it may not feel comfortable. Do not judge yourself. Only sit with the feeling and breathe it in to actualize it. It is a feeling: the feeling is being triggered from your past; it awakens your child Part; and that brings tension into your body. Your child is asking you to pay attention and help.

When you visualize the situation and sense the feelings that are being evoked by the dynamics in that moment, you can begin to understand why this circumstance is causing you to feel a certain way. You can then move into the **alternate thought** phase of going to the SPA.

BUT FIRST . . . **Step 3:**

Assess your intensity. Rate your feeling of anxiety, stress, anger, or sadness on a scale of 1 to 10 with 10 being the highest.

As soon as you become aware of the presence of increased emotional and/or physical intensity, make an initial assessment as to the intensity of those emotions and physical symptoms. Listen to the amount, speed, and volume of the mental chatter.

Scan your body for the level of physical intensity you are experiencing in that moment and combine the awareness of those factors to arrive at the numerical value you can assign to the intensity you are experiencing. This becomes your reference point for when you reflect back on the degree of calm you have restored through this SPA reframing.

Step 4: Alternate thought to be substituted

The A in SPA represents the **alternate thought** that you will create. When you have embraced your feelings as part of you, allowed yourself to be entitled to those feelings without self-judgment, and allowed yourself to own them, you are ready to create an **alternate thought**.

Creating an **alternate thought** will be very personal and specific to the particular situation you are experiencing. In general, self-awareness is needed in order to determine what feeling you are experiencing in reaction to the circumstances.

If what you are feeling stems from a traumatic experience, then that feeling has likely been cut off from your consciousness. Dr. Schwartz identifies that feeling as being "Exiled" and tied to your past. In the current situation it may be felt as anger, injustice, or rejection but the intensity is strong.

Once your recognize that the hurt or anger is tied to something in the past, you can then choose to parent yourself and express your needs in an adult manner to work through the strong emotion.

Jumping ahead to the **alternate thought** step without giving yourself time to do the feeling part will ultimately slow down your learning about yourself and your understanding of why you have certain feelings.

Investing the time now in getting to know yourself will, in the future, allow you to recognize returning emotions more quickly each time the same feelings are aroused. Taking time now will lead to your future efficiency.

How To Create An Alternate Thought?

Look at the particular circumstance you want to reframe through your adult Self's eyes. Take your initial cleansing breath. Below is a list of some of the questions or considerations you can ask yourself when you want to create your **alternate thought**:

1. Try using a word opposite to what was in your mental chatter.

2. If you are feeling angry, ask yourself what needs to be said to the other person that will allow you to be assertive, entitled, in control, clear, valued, worthy, or proud to name a few. Give yourself a **voice**.

3. What words would make the situation feel safe to you?

4. Is there an action you could take, such as not avoiding the situation? Breathe through it and stay present. Do not find an excuse to leave. Stay with the discomfort—it will pass.

5. Ask yourself, "How do I want this to turn out?"

6. If you are feeling hurt or rejected, what needs to change so that you will not feel hurt, rejected, or betrayed?

7. Plug empathy and forgiveness into your thinking when creating your **alternate thought**.

8. When creating your thought—look at both perspectives— yours and that of the other party or parties involved.

9. What are the aspects of the situation that frustrate you? In other words, what person, law, expectation, judgment, or part of the situation is at the core of your frustration? Verbalize what words change that aspect of the situation within you.

Once you have determined the word or phrase that creates the **alternate thought**, literally voice that word or phrase out loud and from your adult Self to all your Parts. Speak your **alternate thought** with firmness, conviction and kindness.

Step 5: Assess your intensity after substituting the **alternate thought**.

Assess the intensity level felt following a reframing technique by initiating a cleansing breath (closing your eyes is optional) and scanning your body for any areas of muscle tension or any of the symptoms identified in the Symptoms of Anxiety table (chapter 3). Assign your level of body tension and emotional distress a numerical figure that represents that intensity level on a scale from 1–10 with 10 representing the highest intensity.

Assessing the intensity level being felt *following* a reframing intervention and comparing it to the pre-reframing level will provide you with the feedback necessary to determine the effectiveness of the intervention as well as indicate if there may be more than one part or component to this stressor that needs to be dealt with in order to more completely reduce your anxiety level satisfactorily.

If the intensity level is still disturbing to you, look for an equally important **pheeling** that may be layered within that circumstance that may not have been attended to. Create an additional **alternate thought** to address the newly recognized feeling. Reframe the circumstance by including the original **alternate thought** in addition to the newly created **alternate thought.** Follow that enhanced intervention with a new assessment of your intensity level.

Reframing will gradually allow you to honor, value, and love yourself for the incredible person you are. You will gain insights from your practice, and this is a monumental accomplishment. Insights will lead to self-acceptance and love for yourself. Knowing yourself is necessary in order for you to protect yourself against anxiety in future situations when angst and doubt fill your mind. Always start with your cleansing breath and adult Self.

Sample situations provided throughout this book will not perfectly match your life. You can extrapolate them to similar situations that have elicited comparable feelings for you in your life.

SPA METHOD—SAMPLE REFRAMING 1

A co-worker at the office is always playing one-upmanship. The co-worker is forever jumping in to take credit for your initiative.

You feel very uncomfortable making a confrontation face-to-face because you envision them turning it around on you and accusing you of being paranoid or stating that it's "all in your head," "I would never do that," or "How could you even think I would do that?" They might state, "I would never take credit where credit is not due."

You suspect they might make this scene obvious to everyone else in the office by making accusations that make you look paranoid and saying them loud enough for everyone to hear. Also, you fear they might use manipulative strategies to turn others against you.

Or perhaps, simply being direct with another person is just a too uncomfortable for you—it is too difficult a task. It creates too risky a feeling in you because of what other workers might think about you. Or perhaps, simply speaking up for yourself is crippling. You simply do not feel equipped to make the confrontation.

Choosing to avoid a confrontation will keep you marching to your old self-beliefs like thinking you are not entitled to speak up and holding onto negative self-judgments, shame, or fear of taking a stand, to name a few. The idea feels very uncomfortable.

Whatever the circumstances, the situation is eating away at you, making you feel unappreciated, filling you with unrest, feelings of helplessness and maybe even anger—all of which is causing you to lose sleep and perhaps even make you feel as if you want to find a new job. You are filled with angst and doubt, which yields internal stress.

Let's Take Anger to the SPA

You will start by taking your cleansing breath to initiate the physiological reduction of stress (chapter 3). Then you will call forth your adult Self to walk you through the five steps.

1. See the feeling

2. Pheel the feeling

3. Assess your intensity of the feeling

4. Alternate thought to be substituted

5. Assess your intensity of the feeling after substituting the new thought

See your anger at being cheated and deceived by your co-worker. Is it red? Is it exploding? Are you running away? Do you have your sword out of its sheath? Take the time to visualize that anger.

Pheel your anger at having your ideas and hard work stolen from you. Pair your feelings to what you are seeing. Does it feel like you are stretched as tight and taut as a rubber band? Do your muscles feel like steel or silly putty? Can you feel heat all over your body? Are you sweating, breathing rapidly, or unable to sit still?

Assess your Intensity: 9

Alternate Thought: you develop the following substitute thought, **"I will not tolerate her abuse. I have a plan to proactively circumvent her success at taking credit for my work."**

You have stated, "I have a plan"—taking action produces energy with which to react, <u>not</u> passively tolerate. Taking action always empowers you and gives you hope.

Your Plan: here is the plan you formulate:

In the future, I will have discussions with several other co-workers and my manager before I get too far along in

planning. I can even distribute emails concerning my ideas and ask people questions. That way there will be several people who will correctly assign the originality of the work to me. I will not share my ideas with Theodora Thief at all.

Assess your intensity: 5.

In general, the allowance you provide for yourself to experience your feelings is exactly what will allow you to move through this technique very quickly and effectively in the future. There is a pattern to our stressors and one situation's resolution can be carried over into future reframing opportunities.

Your desire to eventually use the reframing technique quickly and efficiently in the future can motivate you now to take the time for as much practice as possible. Use the practice to identify your anxious feelings, name them, and acknowledge they are part of you that can be used to promote change within you.

It can take a little time to get to the point where you immediately become self-aware of anxious feelings being evoked, but with practice on your part, you will find yourself experiencing speed and success down the line.

You will immediately be able to jump to the **alternate thought** process without all the analysis. When you accept who you are, you do not need time to rehash the insights. Love yourself and move through it.

SPA METHOD—SAMPLE REFRAMING 2

You get off the phone from a call with your sister, and you feel a familiar angst or stress rising within your body. It occurs to you that this is usually how you feel when finishing a phone call with your sister.

You take a few minutes to register the stress and spend some time attaching feelings to that stress level. You recognize the connection between this stress and previous stress following a call with her. You cognitively may say to yourself, "She always acts like such an authority and disregards my opinion. She doesn't seem to give me any value." Seize this opportunity to reframe!

As always, you start by initiating your cleansing breaths, and then you bring forth your adult Self.

See: I am hurt because it feels like she does not value me. The hurt looks dejected, slumped over, gloomy, and dark. I see the anger: my anger looks red and like a deep river.

Pheel: I feel angry because I have good information and experience, yet she always takes the stage and asserts her opinions. There does not seem to be a point of view other than hers. I recognize she takes on this attitude out of her need to validate herself by appearing like an authority.

It seems we always fall into the childhood pecking order of our ages where I defer to her authority rather than my own. I am angry and frustrated with myself. I do not know how to get her to listen and understand that I have knowledge and valuable experience, too.

Assess your intensity: 7

Alternate thoughts: I do not need my sister's validation. I value my self, and know I have valuable experience and knowledge.

I forgive her. I recognize that I cannot change a person—I can only change myself in relation to that person. If I want to assert my opinion in the future and not remain silent, I can respectfully speak my opinion or idea when she has finished speaking.

I can remind her that there is always more than one way to think about something and that considering all options or ideas will yield making the best choice. I understand I have no control over what she will do with my statement but I know I need to assert myself.

Assess your intensity: 3

It might be important to script out a dialogue for the next time this happens when she calls so that you are prepared when this arises and have confidence to carry it off. You will love yourself afterwards, and the script will allow you to put it away for today. The scripting out exercise will further reduce your intensity level.

SPA METHOD—SAMPLE REFRAMING 3

A financial planner is at your home putting alot of pressure on you to buy into his annuity plan and you would like more time to read through the literature and do some research on the various options available. You are short on time so the urge to sign on the dotted line and be done with it is tempting.

The children need to be put to bed and are causing havoc in the next room. You can feel tension and stress starting to take over and your back and shoulders are aching. It feels like you are about to blow. Suddenly, you remember you have a tool and you take your cleansing breaths.

Assess your Intensity: 7

Alternate thought: No one has a gun to my head—I can give myself more time.

You calmly explain to the agent you will look at everything and get back to him but right now your family comes first. Thank him for his time and advice. You will call him next week.

Assess your Intensity: 3 (You still have all the bedtime duties to work through.)

REFRAMING THROUGH FORGIVENESS

Forgiveness as a reframing technique is valuable in everyday types of situations or as a starting point of discussion when a friend or partner has broken trust in some way. The forgiveness reframing samples in this book, deal with everyday situations.

However, in circumstances where a significant perpetrating act has been experienced, such as sexual abuse, rape, murder, arson, or some other heinous act, the willingness and ability to forgive will be significantly more difficult if possible at all. Professional support could be valuable in working through your anger toward the perpetrator.

Forgiveness, strategy 5, presented in chapter 8, is an essential component of healthy relationships. If you enter every conversation with forgiveness present in your heart, the outcome from that conversation will be better than if forgiveness was not present. Let's explore forgiveness as a reframing method.

Forgiveness is the act of letting go of your hurt emotions so that forward movement can happen. Unfortunately, most people think that in order to forgive there must first be reconciliation, in other words, that the forgiver accepts that the bad deed is now OK—as if it did not matter. That is not forgiveness—that would only be dishonoring your hurt.

There can be no reconciliation until there has been forgiveness. Once the anger or hurt has been experienced and acknowledged, the offended person can make a choice to hang onto those emotions and continue to let them churn inside, or ask their adult Self to help lead them out of the angst by extending forgiveness.

You can decide you have spent enough time holding onto the emotions because you recognize the relationship is more important than your being correct. You recognize there has been no forward movement and that you've been stuck, which is stressful and unhealthy for you.

If and when you feel ready to trust in the forgiveness reframing technique, take an adult cleansing breath and extend unconditional forgiveness—I think you will feel an immediate reduction in body tension.

Take a deep breath in through your nose and exhale loudly through your mouth, releasing and letting go of those emotions. It may take several of these deep breaths to clear your inner atmosphere.

When your body feels more at ease, speak to your "multitudes" (Parts) as referred to in the quote by Walt Whitman in chapter 4. Richard Schwartz recognizes your multitudes as your (Internal Family Systems—IFS) Parts.

Speaking to your Parts, you could saying something like:

I am going to lead us in forgiveness because forgiving will allow all of us to move forward in connection to those we need and want in our life and help to restore balance and happiness to our days. I recognize where and how I have been injured but for the sake of future health and happiness, it is time to move forward in forgiving, we all will experience and benefit from the unifying force of forgiveness.

The release of tension will be felt immediately. You may suddenly notice your breathing is lighter. Hanging onto hurt and disappointment prolongs your angst because it perpetuates the hurt feelings. The feelings reflect your Part's hurt and that indicates they are carrying the "baton" and they perpetuate the tension.

Letting go of your emotions opens the way for reconnection with those you care about. When the hurt has been significant, forgiveness seems like the wrong thing to do because you think it renders you more vulnerable and vulnerability puts into question your entire premise of having to be perfect. It will take a great leap of trust to believe in the power of forgiveness.

Once you give yourself over to the forgiveness process, it will eliminate many of your indecisions (stress) because you will be committing to another pathway. After you have extended forgiveness, rebuilding can begin—prior to forgiveness, the shame and guilt that either party may feel can be too debilitating to open your hearts and believe that forgiveness might be possible. Without trust in the forgiveness process, you both stay stuck in pain.

After extending forgiveness, feelings can be shared. You need to express your hopes and expectations, which must happen before reconciliation can commence. There will be much to be shared and total honesty and respect will be needed. Take your time to plan and talk regularly and frequently. If your hearts agree, reconciliation is possible.

An eye for an eye will make the whole world blind.

—Mahatma Gandhi—

FORGIVENESS—SAMPLE REFRAMING 1

My boyfriend forgot my birthday. I am really disappointed and hurt.

Assess your intensity: 6

Take two cleansing breaths and find your adult Self.

Your adult Self needs to step forward to kindly but firmly say to all your other Parts, "I forgive my boyfriend for forgetting my birthday. When I reminded him it was my birthday, he stated he was so sorry for having forgotten.

Alternate thought: It is more important that we enjoy our time together. If I continue to hold onto my disappointment, it will ruin the remainder of the evening for both of us.

Assess your intensity: 1

FORGIVENESS—SAMPLE REFRAMING 2

My neighbor's dog keeps using our yard as his latrine. My children are forever stepping in the dog poop, and then I have to clean it off their sneakers. I hate that odor, especially when it's in the house—the smell is overwhelming.

Start with a cleansing breath (feel the tension being released) and find your adult Self.

Assess your intensity: 6 to 7

Say hello to your adult Self and take two cleansing breaths. Then from your adult Self tell your other Parts, **"I forgive my neighbors for not having more consideration and better control over their dog."**

Forgiveness: At this point, you might feel that the concept and commitment to forgiveness reframing has adequately reduced your stress. If not, you could combine the Forgiveness reframing with the Understanding Both Perspectives reframing. Remember, your goal is stress reduction, which will protect your physical health. The objective is not about your being "right."

Reconciliation: in the big scheme of life, I understand how life can be very busy, and when my neighbors get home from work after picking up their four kids at school, their dog bounds out of their house before they can grab hold of him because he has been housebound all day.

It is the same in the morning—Buster bounds out of their house because he has been shut up all night. He immediately goes to the nearest familiar spot, which happens to be in our yard. So I understand that they are not purposefully annoying or inconveniencing me. They simply have a lot going on and are not aware of this situation.

You could not have seen this perspective (the reconciliation) if you had not extended forgiveness to your neighbor first.

Assess your intensity: 5

Alternate Thought: I still need to honor my irritation and consider how to handle it.

My wife and I really enjoy them as people. Our kids love playing with their children. The relationships we share with them add a lot of value to our life and family.

If I just forgive them these trespasses, what would that look like? I would still have to work at not letting it bother me.

Reconciliation: what can I do to solve my problem of the sneakers and the dog poop because the benefit of having them as neighbors far outweighs the smell of the dog poop?

I need to work in my own circle. If you do not like the way people are behaving, you need to look at what you can change in your own behavior towards them so that your needs are recognized and respected.

Assess your intensity: 3

Draw a circle around your feet and work on everyone in that circle.

—Watermark Church, Relengage Book—

You have taken control of your inner frustrations by deciding you need to turn your passiveness into action—you will make a plan for communicating your needs.

Adult Plan: I get home earlier in the day than my kids do, and I could take on the job of bagging up the neighbor's dog poop right away before it gets stepped in. It really is not that big a deal for me to remember to do that. I will talk to Andy and Melissa, my neighbors, and tell them how the dog poop is being brought into our house and that I have a plan I would like to try if it is OK with them. This discussion will bring the situation to their attention and it can become a joint effort.

I will wash down the area of the lawn thoroughly. I could transfer the poop to a corner of their yard out of the way and ask them to consistently lead their dog to that spot while giving him the command to, "Go Pee," give him a treat to reinforce the behavior, thereby making the new area Buster's permanent latrine.

If they will unfailingly lead Buster to that spot over the next few months, the habit should be established and then they can resume just letting him out with a command to go to "Go Pee" and he should take himself there.

Talking to Andy and Melissa will let them see I am not angry and that I am willing to take part in the resolution process. This might also get them more involved in helping to train Buster and could provide us both with a lot of laughs. As a matter of fact, talking to anybody without anger can result in them taking their own action to resolve the issue.

Maybe Andy and Melissa will have a plan too.

This effort may or may not work, so I have to be prepared to "let it go" and remember the big picture. My wife and I can also make our children more aware of watching where they step, they can point out the poop to us so we can discard it, and as the children continue to grow, they can also become involved in its removal. Making this problem a *shared* effort takes it solely off of my shoulders.

Assess your Angst: 2

The stress reduction comes because you are honoring your frustration and deciding to share the responsibility of the situation with your neighbors—this is an adult way to deal with the problem.

Forgiveness doesn't excuse their behavior. Forgiveness prevents their behavior from destroying your heart.

—Unknown—

ASKING THE, "WHAT IF . . . QUESTION" REFRAMING METHOD

When we face a dilemma or upsetting situation in life, we often are so close to the ins and outs, as well as the progression of the problem, that we forget to stop and take a breath. We are too wrapped up in the narrative. We forget to try looking at it from a fresh point of view. Viewing the situation from a new perspective is what this reframing technique is all about.

The trick, once again, is to notice when you are feeling the anxiety, mental chatter, or angst beginning to stir within. Take your breath and use your adult Self. If you can learn to use the awareness of the anxiety you are feeling as a cue to take a step back and realize you know how to resolve this problem, you will begin to safeguard your days from so much ruminating and negative energy.

Let's look at two examples to see this reframing technique in action.

"WHAT IF . . . QUESTION"—SAMPLE REFRAMING 1

One friend of mine was burdened with the situation of trying to settle the property estate for her father as far as what to do with his house after he died. The deed to his house was in her name; however, the paperwork that declared her ownership was in her brother's possession, and she was not having success in getting that paperwork back from her brother.

She had accrued over $25,000 in legal fees in this attempt, but still she was no closer to getting it all settled. She tried everything she could think of to get her brother to turn over the document. This was causing her to lose sleep and was filling her days with frustration and anger at the increasing cost of the legal work with no resolution in sight. She felt helpless, frustrated, and angry.

She was focused on the sum of money she wanted to be able to pass along to her grandchildren from the sale of her father's property. That desire to help her grandchildren was all she could see.

So, I asked her, "What if . . . you did not have to think about it any longer?"

Her eyes widened, and she responded, "It would feel wonderful!"

I then asked her how she might make that happen?

So I asked, "How would it feel to just let it go?" Could she simply allow her brother to have the paperwork, send him legal documentation releasing her of any liability or responsibility for the property, and move on in life? Could she turn it totally over to him, stop incurring additional legal expenses, and get it out of her mind to sleep better at night? How would that feel?

I witnessed her transformation before my eyes.

She stated that that was what her daughter had been saying to her for a while.

She left our lunch with a bounce in her stride.

"WHAT IF . . . QUESTION"—SAMPLE REFRAMING 2

I want to share my most frequently used example of asking the "What if . . . Question."

When I become aware that I am focusing on finding fault, blame, or irritation in another person and it is causing me stress, I take a breath in my adult Self. Then I ask myself, "What would my life be like if I did not have this person in my life at all?" It is a sobering question, but it instantly brings me back to reality and an appreciation for the significance of that person in my life.

For example, when nighttime snoring is keeping me awake, I use the "What if . . . question." I recognize that the snoring assures me of his presence and the security in that knowledge allows me to find a restful rhythm in the snoring.

If my gentle poking has not resulted in him turning on his side, I work at placing those sounds in the background rather than in my focus—something like white noise and look for my love for this person to fill my heart and bring me peace. The snoring usually does not last that long.

I reframe my angst away from my irritation while simultaneously recognizing what I truly want in my heart. I am thankful for another day with that person in my life.

*Change the way you see things,
and things you see will change.*

—Wayne Dyer—

BACK-DOOR APPROACH REFRAMING

As previously explained (chapter 9), the back-door approach to reframing works as if you are looking back over your shoulder after having already navigated the stress. It's called the back-door approach because it portrays a feeling of friendly calm that is experienced by choosing how you want to feel when the stressful situation concludes.

Stephen Covey lists "Determine Your End Goal" as the second habit in his bestseller the *Seven Habits of Highly Effective People*. He recommends setting a goal by beginning with how you want to visualize the outcome and then back fitting the pieces to make that happen.

The back-door approach focuses on the final outcome first— then plugs in the appropriate actions and attitude for the intervening steps that are entirely aimed at producing that final objective. When we know the outcome, it eliminates apprehension of the unknown—the fear.

If you are familiar enough to visit a friend and enter and exit through their back door, then you are probably very comfortable with that friend, trust the relationship, and that is exactly the feeling you are looking for in stress reduction.

Because reframing will be your new best friend, you will sense the confidence and comfort that comes with relying on this technique of choosing the desired result first. You can trust in the results.

Using this technique where you start by deciding and focusing on the desired end result saves you time from sorting through potential options. It connects you immediately with your heart, gives you a clear objective, and stops the mental ricocheting back and forth between options, choices, and doubt. In this way it provides instant clarity.

The desired result likely will be very clear to you because the worries and the frozen-in-doubt moments have been totally removed. You have jumped past the feelings of angst and are reaching for what your heart desires and that always bring calm.

Searching your heart always paves the way for clear action. After all, your heart is your true friend—it is your

Self. Reframing by coming out of the back door makes the decision process very black and white without any doubt or areas of gray. This is my favorite, most used, and quickest method of reframing.

Let's review how it works by looking at some examples.

BACK-DOOR APPROACH—SAMPLE REFRAMING

Let's say Nancy is approached at a party by someone she has never met previously, and he asks her if they could go out together. Nancy feels drawn to this new man but also recognizes she does not know anything about him. She wonders if it would be safe to accept a date with someone she just met.

Nancy can initiate a couple of deep breaths and bring forth her adult Self. She can go at his invitation through the back door by asking herself, "How will I spend my evening if I do not accept this date? How do I want to feel looking back on the evening?"

The activities that would come to her mind would be routine activities that would be very expected and familiar to her. So, the choice boils down to: does she want a new adventure with this person who seems interesting, or does she want to fall into her familiar activities which are comfortable and safe? She needs to assess where her energy level is and what desire is in her heart.

By examining the two potential outcomes for the evening, the question has been simplified. She is not being distracted by the variables and conditions, such as where to meet this man and would she be safe? She can isolate the variables and conditions, put them aside to return to later, and address those after she connects to her heart to see what she wants to do.

Having seen what truly lies in her heart—to enjoy a new adventure—she can determine the variables and conditions that must be met in order for her to remain safe. She will be coming from a position of strength, not angst, because she will see clearly what her heart wants—and there is great strength in that knowledge.

By setting the variables for safety, she can create a good safe scenario. She can set the date up to keep it safe. The date could be set in group situations or public places so that this first encounter will not place her at risk. It turns the apprehension of the evening into something to be anticipated with excitement and not an evening to be feared.

If Nancy had accepted the date without allowing herself the time to process her feelings through the back-door approach, her enjoyment and excitement of anticipating an adventurous evening would not have been fully experienced because she would have spent all the anticipatory time in a state of turmoil. There would have been too many doubts and worries that would have overshadowed the excitement and adventure.

The back-door approach in this case, Nancy's predetermination of how she wants to spend her evening, eliminates the "What if I do?" versus "What if I don't?" phenomena. She has separated her desires from her fears and answered her heart-felt objective. With that energy and clarity, Nancy will address the variables and conditions.

Imagine the many occasions in which you could use this technique. The list is endless. I think the back-door approach may become your most efficient method of reframing after you have spent practice time connecting with your heart through the SPA method.

Knowing what is in your heart ("Heart Intelligence") will enable you to see and feel your true desires quickly and clearly and that will make this your most efficient method of reframing as time goes on.

You can reframe any question or situation by approaching it from the desired end-result of the situation. Then you base your decisions on where it is you want to end up. If you look at everything from the initial presentation of the circumstances, there are too many factors and considerations. The clarity is often just not there and you can get caught up in the mental muddle of worry, which totally distracts you from the matters of your heart.

BACK-DOOR APPROACH—PRACTICE EXERCISE

With the new awareness of yourself, you are beginning to reevaluate the role your husband has assigned to you over many years when he goes into a rage. You are now seeing that your offering to help your husband when he is frustrated has placed you in close proximity to him which has provided him with the opportunity to transfer his anger onto you (blame you) rather than face his self-beliefs and deal with the source of his anger. He avoids that work by making you his scapegoat.

In the past, when he has encountered a frustration, he has regularly directed his rage at you when you have heard his distress and come to offer help or inquire what's wrong. He has always apologized and felt badly afterwards, but there has not been a reduction in frequency, intensity, or length of outburst.

If they do it often, it isn't a mistake,
it's just their behavior.

—Dr. Steve Maraboli—

But today is a new day and you have gained confidence in dealing with anxiety. You recognize he has made you feel diminished and you have become his whipping post. You have been his scapegoat allowing him to restore his equilibrium while having you carry the responsibility for his frustration.

You completely understand that he does not intentionally do this and that it is his in-the-moment rage (childlike Part) that has taken over and is lashing out at the nearest person. You decide you are tired of this treatment and want to work within yourself to begin to reset his behavior and make him equally aware of the on-going dynamics.

I can't control your behaviors,
nor do I want that burden . . .
but I will not apologize for
refusing to be disrespected,
to be lied to, or to be mistreated.
I have standards,
step up or step out.

—Dr. Steve Maraboli—

Knowing your husband loves you very much, that he truly does not like his behavior, and that he would like to know how to overcome these outbursts, you feel energized to work together. Looking at this scenario from your adult Self and using the back-door approach, you know you can talk with him to bring this habit to a more reasonable conclusion.

Ask yourself, "What is my desired outcome? How do I want to go forward in these circumstances from here on out? What do I want from him? What are reasonable expectations for how I can help? What does he need to become aware of? How long should it take for this new behavior to become the norm?"

Your adult Self understands that accusation, anger, or hurt directed at him from your Part will not accomplish true communication nor a productive exchange of ideas.

Take the time to put together how you would want the dialogue to look. Employ empathy, forgiveness, and leadership.

Answer the previous questions to yourself in order to gain clarity. Then make a list of statements for your spouse followed by your questions as demonstrated in chapter 8. Make sure you set realistic expectations and WRITE THEM OUT ON PAPER.

You can modify this exercise to more accurately represent a situation in your life by putting in different cast members, different dynamics or changing the situation. Somewhere in your life you have a relational problem that would benefit from setting up new expectations and boundaries.

The heart is a muscle, and you strengthen muscles by using them. The more I lead with my heart, the stronger it gets.

—Mark Miller—

UNDERSTANDING BOTH PERSPECTIVES REFRAMING

Another technique for reframing is to view a situation from the other person's perspective—from the outside looking in. Following all of your mindfulness and insightfulness practice, you can look at yourself as other people see you.

You can decide how you want to be viewed and tailor your demeanor, attitude, and approach from that perspective. Using this approach for stress reduction is a little slower or more involved, but it still works very well. It requires a very adult Self.

SEEING BOTH PERSPECTIVES—SAMPLE 1

The seeing-both-perspectives reframing technique works in combination with the SPA reframing technique. To understand how it works, let's follow as it is used in the next example.

Let's say you are discussing a work project at the office with a co-worker. You have a difference of opinion about the sequence of steps to be taken, and you both seem to be confident in your respective proposed method. You are sensing tension between the two of you, so—**STOP.**

Remember the discussion in chapter 6 about micro-communications when you are sensing tension during a conversation? More than likely both participants are in their Protector Parts and it is those unproductive Protector Parts that are engaging with each other, rather than the two adult Self's of you and your co-worker. To reduce the tension and anxiety, you must activate your adult Self.

Self-awareness tells you to take a cleansing breath to initiate stress reduction and to activate your adult Self. If you need a little more space, excuse yourself for a personal call and assure them you will be right back. This will also allow them time to take a step back.

Assess your tension: 6 (Remember to make a quick mental note of this level.)

Next mindfully work to "see both perspectives" by considering what the other person might be feeling in this exact shared moment of your conversation. Do you think the co-worker may also be frustrated? If so, then you are having a *shared* experience. *Shared* denotes a connection between you both!

With your adult Self in control, create the **alternate thoughts** to productively move through the situation.

For example, some **alternate thoughts** might be: **Greater progress will be made if we put our adult heads together. I could identify our mutual frustration, so we can laugh together because ultimately we both are committed to**

the same goal. Together, we can make this a congenial meeting.

Assess your tension: 5

Discussions or confrontations are a normal part of human interactions. It is unrealistic to think that they do not occur even within the best marriages, partnerships, work places, friendships, or families.

They are a healthy characteristic of any relationship so long as each person comes to the table with understanding, compassion, and an open heart. All parties need to feel heard and valued.

Chances are the other person is equally disturbed by the words that were exchanged or the palpable tension between you both. If you assess they are equally disturbed, then you can trust that they are giving you the same value you are giving to them. (That is also an **alternate thought** that puts a positive spin on your understanding.)

From this place of seeing both perspectives, create another **alternate thought**:

Each of us cares about what the other thinks. You'll realize it feels pretty good when you reframe the disagreement in this light.

Assess your tension: 3

You have reframed the focus of feeling hurt or angry to knowing that you are valued and respected and that you value and respect the other person. You are sharing an experience and are connected to one another. These are all powerful **alternate thoughts**.

Suddenly, the atmosphere feels lighter and brighter because you have considered the other person's perspective and changed what is in your heart, let go of the fear or anger, and are thinking about forgiveness and the shared project-oriented connection, which allows you to move forward together.

Assess your tension: 1

SEEING BOTH PERSPECTIVES SAMPLE 2

Say Jon calls and leaves you a voicemail. In a roundabout way, he invites you out to dinner for the night. He states, "This is Jon," and proceeds to say, "I don't have anything much to do tonight, so I thought we could hang out together and catch a bite to eat. Please call me back."

Because of the nonchalant and demeaning way Jon framed the invitation, even though you would like to spend time with him, you find his invitation leaves you feeling pretty flat. Perhaps, you even feel a stirring inside that reflects some anger at the insulting way he has slung the invitation at you.

STOP.

This is where you register the stirring feeling inside, embrace it, harness it, and plug in a reframing technique to transform it into calm.

See it. Take a breath to identify that you are feeling something. Sad, disappointed, not valued, annoyed, angry—can you see the anger or humiliation you are experiencing? Does it have a color? Is it bright or dark? Is it room temperature? Is it prickly or smooth?

Pheel it. Label the emotion by naming it—let's say it is lack of value—and allow yourself to really feel it.

Jon's choice of words may have provoked anger, hurt, or a feeling in you of being undesirable. You need to acknowledge the feeling that his words provoked in you. Acknowledge it, name it, and recognize how you are feeling.

Now feel the hurt, anger, or undesirability. What does it do to your body? Do you slouch? Do you shuffle your feet? Are you hanging your head or perhaps shaking it back and forth from left to right? Recognize how that makes you feel—not appreciated. Is it painful? Do you feel like shouting or stomping your feet in protest? Are you pacing?

Assess your intensity: 7 to 8

When you can **see** the disappointment and unrest, **pheel** the lack of value and the effect that it has on you, it is time to substitute an **alternate thought** to transform your perspective so that you can more clearly see what actions or options you can "choose to select" in order to move forward.

Alternate thought: Consider this invitation was *intended* to be a compliment.

Assess your intensity: 6

With this possibility in mind, examine the situation from the other person's perspective. Stepping forward with your adult Self, look at the situation from both perspectives.

Let's look at your knowledge of Jon.

1. Is Jon outgoing, does he exude confidence, and find conversation easy? No.
2. Is Jon a fellow who dates frequently? No.
3. Do you consider Jon to be a cool guy? No.

From trying to view the situation from Jon's perspective you surmise—Jon probably did not make a proper invitation because he was trying to disguise the invitation in such a way so that if you said you were busy, he would not be as personally injured and embarrassed.

Assess your intensity: 5

Now let's say yes to all three questions: Jon is a really cool guy who is confident, has plenty of dates, and is easy to be with because he is a great conversationalist.

Based on your positive assessments of Jon, you are interested in a bite to eat with him, but he definitely did not make you feel very desirable. So you would like to say yes,

BUT you want to make it clear to him that you expect more respect. In this way you listen to what your heart wants, but you must decide how to handle Jon's ineptness.

So, if Mr. Cool Jon called to suggest spending time together making the proposal in a properly worded invitation, that would mean that he values you and thinks a casual evening with you would be nice. This type of invitation piques your interest and flatters you.

The comparison of these two proposals makes it clear to you that if you do agree to his "bite to eat," you need to explain to him what you would expect for proposed plans in the future.

Assess your intensity: 4

What if Jon is kind of a quiet guy, who has to work hard to converse and, as far as you know, does not have lots of dates, then would it be a compliment that he mustered up his courage to call you at all? I suspect you might say yes.

Alternate thought:

Jon was taking a big risk to call me. From Jon's perspective, it was a big deal and he meant it sincerely.

With this **alternate thought** you can appreciate his risk-taking. You can see that he is eager to spend some time with you even though his social skills are lacking.

Assess your intensity: 4

Since the final resolution to this situation is still not firmly set in your mind, the intensity of your unrest has not diminished. You need to determine your final desire by visiting what is in your heart in order to be clear and be able to move through the resolution.

Reevaluate: Jon is either both shy and uncomfortable calling to ask you out and that comes across in his poor social graces, or he is competent but lacking in social graces. If he is competent but a jerk socially, are you interested in spending time with him? If he is shy and uncomfortable, do you want to encourage a relationship with him, or do you want to say no?

In either case, you have to look into your heart and determine your desires. Do not let other people's judgments of Jon alter the feelings in your heart. Can you see how we have combined two reframing techniques—seeing both perspectives and the back-door approach?

In either case, if you say yes, then can you see clearly it is your feeling of being devalued that is continuing to maintain the stress?

You know that you need to address future invitations from Jon because you do not want to feel undesirable in the future. You need to know that this will not be a recurring issue. Jon needs to know your expectations, so he can be accountable.

In no way should you not protect your hurt Parts and disregard how his words made you feel. You would not want him to repeat this feeble attempt at an invitation again in the future, so giving Jon feedback as to how he made you feel is important.

Assess your intensity: 3 (You are gaining more clarity in what you want and what you need to do.)

For the sake of following through on this scenario, let's say you are interested in going out with Jon. Therefore, you need to let him know your invitation expectations so that your relationship does not begin with a bad habit. Because relationships are so easily compromised over communication skills, you should start out by exercising those and getting off on the right foot.

This may feel very risky or uncomfortable but work through it with your adult Self, dialoguing one step at a time until it feels like something you can risk asserting. Experimenting will begin to set you free.

You could overlook your hurt, which I strongly do not recommend because your hurt Parts will not learn to trust you—and your Parts must be able to trust you as if you are their parent leading them to resolution.

Your choices might be:

1) "Yeah sounds great—can't wait—what time?"

This response will not allow Jon to understand the impact of his word choices and will not encourage him to grow from the experience. Additionally this response disregards your reaction to his clumsiness and your hurt.

2) "Jon, by your choice of words, I get the feeling you are considering me as a last resort for your evening's entertainment—is that a correct assumption?"

By asking Jon this honest question, you will tap into Jon's adult Self, asking his adult Self to be accountable. You will invite Jon to take another try at his wording. This response also honors your hurt and provides strong leadership by your adult Self.

3) "Jon, you are a nice guy, and the idea of sharing the evening with you is interesting to me. If you could present your idea as a positive, clear invitation, I probably would feel very eager to say yes."

In this response, you start with a compliment and then go directly to the point of contention, all the while indicating a shared evening would be agreeable. This shows respect to Jon and, most importantly, honors your feelings and need for respect.

Jon, whether or not he is Mr. Cool or Mr. Humble Pie, will appreciate that you honestly explained how you felt. If he truly wants to share an evening with you, he would feel terrible if his word choice blew away the prospects for that happening.

Jon could learn a valuable lesson from you—that words do

have meaning and that he needs to learn to "mean what he says and say what he means." He will probably never make that mistake again. Jon will look at you with great value because you are giving yourself great value.

If you do not want to go out with Jon, it doesn't matter that much what words you select but using empathetic consideration of his feelings would be more graceful.

4) Tell Jon to go fly a kite.

This would bring retribution to you but embarrassment to Jon. It might allow you to feel powerful, but any chance of sharing time with Jon now or in the future would be negated.

> *Blowing out someone else's candle doesn't make yours shine any brighter.*
>
> —Unknown—

5) Finally, if you do not care to go out with Jon tonight or in the future, explain that you do have something to do tonight but thank him for the thought.

This is a polite response that implies you would rather not spend time with him.

Assess your intensity: 2

Stepping back, taking a breath, and assessing a stressful situation calmly in your adult Self will bring a certain level of calm just by allowing yourself some reflective time.

REALITY-CHECK REFRAMING METHOD

Taking a reality check of a situation can lead to reframing the circumstance you feel conflicted and anxious about. By taking a reality check of what is actually happening, you may be able to sort through the issues more clearly.

The reality check could provide an **alternate thought** that might transform your doubts and fears into confidence. Let's read through an example to see how the reality check reframing technique works.

REALITY-CHECK REFRAMING SAMPLE 1

In chapter 3, I stated I live with social anxiety. When I am at a social function where I have expressed ideas, I find myself ruminating after the party about how I sounded, if people minded my speaking, or whether or not they respected or valued what I contributed. I worry they will go home thinking I am a bore or I am a nut.

My ruminations will keep me from falling asleep at night while tossing and turning as I reflect on how I was perceived by people at the party. I relive the scenes over and over again. I fall into the judge-and-jury role as my mental chatter takes over.

I have learned to reframe my ruminations when this happens and transform the negative mental chatter into peaceful acceptance, which allows me to then fall off to sleep.

So, join me for a minute in my nocturnal tossing and turning: all kinds of judgments and questions are passing through my mind, creating loud and confusing mental chatter.

By practicing mindfulness, I become self-aware of what I am doing to myself. Mindfulness and self-awareness bring me back into the present moment, and I understand and see how I am causing myself to lose sleep.

I am turning that nice social gathering into my nightmare (the ghost my mind is drawing). I see the angst that my mental chatter is evoking and connect my feelings to how that makes me feel in the present moment. I am rejecting myself and devaluing my opinion or the information that I would like to share with friends or acquaintances.

So, I start with a cleansing breath and my adult Self.

See: I **see** the rejection of myself. It looks gray, sluggish, and I am hiding in shame.

My doubt about providing value to other people is eating me up. This self-awareness allows me to recognize what I am doing to myself. I am able to connect my feeling of not having value at tonight's party to childhood feelings of not feeling valued in my family or with friends.

I need to halt the mental chatter and examine what I am seeing and what my thoughts are causing me to feel. Self-awareness is seeing yourself in the reality of the mindfulness moment you are in—which presents you with a moment of choice.

Pheel: I feel a rejection of myself, and I feel lonely and sad. Lacking entitlement to have a voice makes me feel as if I do not have the same rights as other people, and that makes me feel different, angry and misunderstood. Doubts about my value to others cause me to feel inferior, unworthy and ashamed. I have felt these feelings before; they are very familiar to me. I feel as I did when I was a child growing up.

Assess your intensity: 8

Childhood feelings were exactly what I was feeling. Mindfulness in this moment engages my self-awareness, and that self-awareness allows me to see myself as a child experiencing my perception of childhood rejection.

The voices are my old friends admonishing me for having shared my ideas—exposing me to judgment or criticism. I say, "Hello" to my inner friends and choose to reframe.

I acknowledge these old feelings but because I have visited these feelings so thoroughly in the past, I do not need to linger with them. Instead, I call forward my adult Self to lead me forward through the tossing and turning that is keeping me awake.

My child Part is not capable of leading me with clarity. I need to be an adult. I need to clear the confusion and voices of my multiplicity.

At this point I have asked my adult Self to step forward and lead me through the reframing technique. I will not experience resolution through the reality check method of reframing without being in my adult Part.

Alternate thought: I choose to recall my memory of the party as it really happened. This is the reality I recall:

1. I did not stand by myself at all during the evening
2. I was in continuous conversation with different groups or individuals all night
3. I never saw people using body language that indicated boredom as if they were not interested or not eager to connect
4. I do remember that almost everyone in the group was contributing to the discussion

That is my reflection on the reality of what took place during the party.

Assess your intensity: 2

I take several cleansing breaths, recognize I am returning to my old negative beliefs, and understand I need to forgive myself for allowing my childhood rules to enter my thinking process and dominant my thoughts—I need to "Let them go." Sleep comes because I allow for self-acceptance.

REALITY-CHECK REFRAMING SAMPLE 2

Let's say your parents would like to have you come for a visit. They have not seen you in a year and are putting pressure on you to fit in a visit during your spring break from school when you will be off from teaching.

You understand their need to see you; however, one of your fellow teachers suggested a road trip together to a neighboring state to see an exhibit that is being shown around the country in various cities. Your co-worker also suggested that you combine seeing the exhibit with a couple of days at a beach cottage where you both could get some real downtime, walk the beach, eat out, and truly unwind.

You are feeling pressure to conform to your parent's request, which would require an airline ticket, and that would be difficult to pull out of your budget. You are excited about the trip idea with your co-worker and you would be able to drive and split the cost between the two of you.

Now what do you do? How do you not hurt your parents' feelings or disappoint your fellow teacher when she is counting on your companionship and cost-sharing so that both of you have a nice spring break week without breaking the bank? How do you determine what it is that you truly want to do?

The guilt and anxiety start to tour your mind, and pretty soon you have on-going mental chatter keeping you from focusing on your papers to correct and making it difficult for you to fall asleep or stay asleep throughout the night.

Your mind is beset with guilt and doubt as to how to make the choice. It is interfering with your concentration and ability to finish correcting papers.

STOP . . . Take a cleansing breath, harness the anxiety energy, call forth your adult Self, and make a reality check list by listing the pros and cons of each choice.

Reality Check—Exhibit/Beach Cottage:

1. +You can afford the week away with your co-worker.
2. + It would be fun and relaxing.
3. + It would be a new adventure.
4. + It fits into your budget.
5. + It is exciting to think about.

   6. + You are burned-out and need a real restful break.

Reality Check—Visit Parents:

   1. + It would be nice to see your parents.

   2. + Visiting with your parents would make them happy.

   3. + Visiting with your parents would take away your feelings of guilt.

   4. + You love your parents.

   5. + You do not want to hurt their feelings.

   6. − Your parents would be asking all kinds of probing questions.

   7. − The airfare to the West Coast is more than your budget can handle.

   8. − It is predictable, not an adventure.

   9. − It is not always relaxing.

Looking at the pros and cons to each vacation option gives you a tally. There are six positive reasons to go with your co-worker and no negatives. There are five positive reasons to visit your parents and four negative considerations. Three of the five positive reasons for visiting your parents serve their needs, not yours.

Making the list brings the REALITY of the situation and your desires into clear view: the exhibit and beach cottage is the choice for you.

Now the questions are how to handle it so as not to be filled with guilt, and how to break it to your parents.

Reality Check—Presentation:

   1. Your parents should love you no matter what.

   2. Your parents are capable of understanding your need to maintain a budget.

   3. Ask your parents for help with the airline ticket price so that you could buy it far in advance at a much lower price.

   4. A summer visit would be longer, and you would enjoy visiting with them so much more if it could be a longer stay

and not rushed by the constraints of the weeklong break.

5. Because the summer vacation provides more flexibility in time, you could plan to take a small trip together while you are out there.

6. The small excursion together would turn the visit into an adventure with your parents, and it could be fun.

7. You could share expenses.

8. There are so many wonderful places to see in California.

9. If you plan this trip now, you can get lower airfare prices and really have fun making plans together over the phone in the upcoming months, which would help to build the excitement and momentum.

The exercise of listing the different perspectives, attitudes, etc., provides a quantitative analysis of the predicament. Notice that the task of telling your parents now seems more comfortable and your guilt and anxiety has been tremendously reduced. Plus, you can see some benefits of spending time with your parents.

They will love to hear that you would prefer not to come at this time because it is only a quick week and is too short a visit for the expensive airfare. Plus, they will love to hear that you would like more time with them. With their excitement over the alternate plan, you all can start to engage in making summer plans.

Assess your intensity: 2

Making a reality-check list provides you with a tally sheet on paper to streamline the decision-making process. In turn, this deflates the fear component, clarifies your inner needs and desires, and increases your confidence. It eliminates your inner turmoil by causing you to slow down, allowing you to focus on the situation, which simplifies the arguments so you can see clearly which choice makes the most all-around sense.

When our heads are so full of chatter, we don't fully form

complete thoughts in our minds—only fragments of thoughts. We cannot navigate the doubts and fears because there is too much white noise contributing to the feeling of panic or the feeling of being rushed or pressured.

A reality-check list analyzes and simplifies the decision process. The reality check allows you to slow down and sort out your desires from your feelings so that a sensible plan can be sketched out that satisfies everybody's needs.

Perception is relative, and reality, as it turns out, may be mind-made.

—Deepak Chopra—

GIVING IT TO GOD REFRAMING
A Variation for Faith-based Readers

This final reframing variation is a faith-based method for calming anxiety, doubt, and mental chatter. Turning your faith toward God's love and wisdom allows you to trust and believe in God's ultimate plan.

1. Close your eyes.
2. Take a breath.
3. Pray.
4. Assess your tension level.

Any words in your prayer will be heard so long as it comes from your heart, addresses your concerns, and connects you in partnership and a relationship with God.

Here is an example of giving-it-to-God reframing:

First, close your eyes.

Then, take a long, slow cleansing breath.

Extend your prayer:

Father God, I need to walk with you in life. It is time for me to open my heart fully to that potential. I am asking you to help me learn to trust in the relationship we share together.

I rejoice in your presence and I will demonstrate my faith and belief in you by handing my worries and fears over to you. When I feel unrest, I will put my trust in you. I am asking you to speak to me, and I will turn my attention to your message. I need you in my life. I want to get to know you and spend time with you.

I will approach you in confidence because I know you came to us in the form of Jesus who experienced emotions just like when I experience emotions. You will understand what I am struggling with.

I am asking for you to partner with me as I turn my fears over to you. I believe you have blessed me with the abilities to navigate life using adult capabilities and letting go of my child-like desires, but I know this is a lot to do on my own. Help me to see clearly and feel accurately when my hurt Parts are causing me to detour from my heart—I will listen and return to you.

As I travel with you in partnership, I ask for reminders of what is within my boundaries of control, and I ask for your continued wisdom as we walk together. I will gain a deeper understanding of who you are and what you hope for from me.

I thank you, God, for giving me your grace and allowing me to journey in your path. Amen.

Assess your intensity.

Spending time with God puts everything else in perspective.

—PictureQuotes.com—

Chapter Wrap-up

In this chapter, you have encountered different types of reframing methods:

> ➤ The "Going to the SPA" Reframing Technique

> ➤ Reframing Through Forgiveness

> ➤ Asking the "What If . . . Question" Reframing Method

> ➤ Back-door Approach Reframing

> ➤ Understanding Both Perspectives Reframing

> ➤ Reality-Check Reframing Method

> ➤ Giving It to God Reframing—A Variation for Faith-based Readers

You may choose to employ a single technique or combine techniques. All techniques begin with the same foundation: first recognizing your own feelings of anxiety or discomfort by using self-awareness; next taking a grounding cleansing breath to initiate your physiological calming; and then calling on your adult Self to lead you through the reframing method of your choice. Reframing can be modified to fit individual needs.

By practicing these reframing techniques today, you will begin to form the neural pathways that will become your future pattern for handling stressors and stabilizing a functional approach to your life.

Your Action Plan

> ➤ I have listed some sample stressful situations to be used as practice exercises in the Reframing Exercises and Supplemental Information Packet as a complimentary companion to this book—click here: http://bit.ly/ReframeExercise

> ➤ The free refillable SPA Template is accessible here: http://bit.ly/ReframeSPA

> ➤ The exercises will provide more practice examples for you to work through and help you feel more comfortable with the various reframing methods to jump start your establishment of those new neural pathways in your brain that will change your approach to life.

> If things seem a little slow, we could facilitate the process together.

Chapter 11 will discuss how your inner beliefs are contrived and how they distort our reality. We will summarize this holistic plan, reviewing and tying together the 8 building-block strategies that will significantly contribute to the success of your personal growth and support the primary tool in this book—the reframing technique.

Chapter 11

Time for a New Roadmap

*The present moment is filled with joy
and happiness. If you are present,
you will see it.*

—Thich Nhat Hahn—

This chapter presents an examination of how circumstances affect your developmental world. It presents essential material to help round out your understanding of possible insights into the origins of your stress and anxiety so that you can find the most effective **alternate thought** to use in your reframing techniques that will most effectively and efficiently reduce your tensions.

In addition, chapter 11 will review how the strategies link together to form this holistic blueprint for change. *Reframe Your Viewpoints* provides you with a new roadmap for going forward in life. You have been committed to finishing this book—that dedication is what will bring you payback.

By reviewing and linking together all the components, we will refresh the important rationale, background information, and suggested practices presented in earlier chapters. I believe bringing the components back into focus will boost your understanding, commitment, energy, and enthusiastic planning for the practice of your skills so that you will gain the most from your practice.

You have invested your valuable time in reading *Reframe Your Viewpoints* and you are close to putting everything together to start this journey to entitlement and freedom. A quick review of how everything works and fits together is essential to your ability to remember the details of the treasure map I have laid out for you.

As our lives evolve over time and as we age from one decade into the next, it becomes apparent we need to shift our perspectives and goals to meet the demands for our ever-changing lives. This roadmap can help you organize that pathway.

No matter where you are, what type of change you wish to bring to your life, or what stage of life you are in, there is a basic process to creating change in your life: persistent self-awareness; self-exploration, cognitive goal setting, and habit formation.

Negative Core Beliefs and Traumas

We cannot become what
we want to be by
remaining what we are.

—Max Depree—

While core beliefs can be positive and empowering, for those of us experiencing a lot of stress, tension, and anxiety, it is likely that a number of our core beliefs are crippling—contributing to our high levels of stress. Where on earth do these negative self-beliefs come from that agitate our minds and fill them with mental chatter?

They come from perceptions we establish about ourselves based on the environments we grew up in, people's judgments of us, or negative past experiences. These negative judgments may have come from words used by people who did not think about the cost of their words on small or growing children (children base their self-worth on their interpretations of others' feedback and the dynamics of their environments).

Dan Barber, author of *Parenting From Prison: 5 Lessons from Kids Behind Bars*, interviewed incarcerated adolescents and listened to them reflect on the parenting styles they grew up with. Here's a short list of his significant findings:

1. There was a consensus that parents treated them like objects or pawns without concern for their feelings.

2. Sarcasm was a form of communication used by many of the parents—as young children, it was confusing and they did not understand it. Sarcasm does not reflect love and tenderness.

3. Adult expectations were put on them at a very young age.

4. The home base wasn't a safe place, and the youth questioned why their parents and grandparents openly used drugs in the home.

5. They resented that their parents disciplined them for expectations and rules that they were never taught.

6. They agreed discipline is necessary and benefits children—there is a rationale and safety component to discipline. But they felt they received punishment, which was harsh, punitive, and often not tied to any circumstance. It seemed to satisfy a parent's needs—nothing positive came out of the punishment.

Core beliefs develop from circumstances that threaten and shake a child's stability—as the circumstances in the above list describe. These circumstances result in self-doubt, ridicule, and shame in the child and will lead to an almost impenetrable set of core beliefs, self-doubts, and negative assessments owned by the child and carried into their adulthood. Unfortunately, we see all sensory information through the lens of our core story.

Core beliefs reside within each of us that are based on our core story. We continue to interact with life through our understanding of our core story and who we believe we are until we become aware of and question its validity, strength, and the harmful impact it perpetuates upon our lives. Thankfully, dismantling core beliefs is possible, albeit difficult.

The impact of our total environment contributes to form our perceptions. Our perceptions become the lens from which we view the world, and lenses "crafted" in an unstable and negative environment frequently distort reality. If we fixate on our childhood core story, we give it power over us.

We carry those perceptions and experiences with us through life embedded in the cells of our bodies until we wake up to their presence and take the time to explore them, challenge those beliefs, and parent ourselves in the process of replacing the old beliefs with beliefs based on today's reality.

One way in which to dismantle your core story is to understand that your story was derived from a child's viewpoint. You can remember what your need was but can you remember if anyone else at that time had needs that you might not have been aware of? At that time, could there have been some pressures or demands on the adult(s) in your core story and for some reason (right or wrong), those pressures or demands were given a higher priority than your needs?

As a child, you interpreted adult decisions or behaviors as a reflection of your self worth. Children idealize their parents so allowing parents to be anything other than correct or perfect is outside the normal expectation of a child's mind. Therefore, the child assumes a self-deficiency and interprets the situation as being about a deficiency in them, turning that into a negative self-belief or core story about where they are lacking.

My point is to bring to the table a way for you to start to unravel your negative belief to understand it is was not based on who you are but on the circumstances that created that belief. The interpretations you assign to an event, rather than the actual event itself, determines its effect on your emotions.

Could there be another viewpoint to consider in your core story? Could there be a viewpoint that might relieve you of your perceived wrongdoing? Our core stories keep us imprisoned with our child-like needs and child-like viewpoint leading to sadness or depression. Re-examining our core stories may create a significant shift in our thinking.

Humans hold onto negative experiences, messages, trauma, and the roles that are played out in family dynamics. Those roles are accepted and maintained without question because, as children, we are expected to fit in. In order to maintain stability and avoid judgment, criticism or potential harm during development, we conceptually establish self-construed guidelines to live by, which end up limiting our creativity, spontaneity, and potential.

This book is about reframing your viewpoints. Is it possible your core story could be amended a bit to take in the adult's perspective and needs so that you can begin to understand that your hurt was *not* connected to a deficiency in you? It was connected to the adult's selfish needs, inappropriate behaviors, motivations, disregard for boundaries, or their not attending to a child's safety. Your hurt originated through adults who either could not see your needs or give your needs a higher priority than their own.

Is it time to rewrite the end of your core story? The process of reframing is one way in which to start that exploration. The regular use of reframing contributes to our understanding of the many misperceptions we live by. Gaining insights into your anxiety can initiate the process of replacing old beliefs with beliefs based on truth. Reframing will initiate that change in your life.

We live in societies where a generalized imbalance in power exists. Power imbalances exist between an employer or manager and the worker; between the teacher and the student; between the parent and the schoolteacher or vice versa; between the police officer and the civilian; between TSA personnel and the traveler. The list of power imbalances is endless.

The greatest imbalance of all, however, is between the parent/caregiver and the child because the child is dependent upon the parent/caregiver for their survival. The imbalance is exacerbated further because the child feels a need to please the parent/caregiver so as not to compromise their survival or need for love.

The child will sacrifice their own needs in order to meet the parent's needs. The child's need to please the adult, coupled with the power imbalance, creates a double-whammy effect—the child's perceived need to please the adult overrides the child's original need or desire for security, safety, or basics in life.

Growing up always takes place in an environment where there exists some degree of a power imbalance. If the power imbalance is resilient, then questioning, challenging, or using initiative may not be encouraged, let alone tolerated. It is difficult to achieve wholeness and autonomy under suppression.

Self-Imposed Safety Rules

Throughout development, messages impact children greatly because children cannot process them accurately. Children develop beliefs and safety rules based upon the visualized, verbalized, and underlying messages they are left to interpret.

When you fight yourself to discover the real you, there is only one winner.

—Stephen Richards—

Six Basic Human Needs

Tony Robbins identifies Six Basic Human Needs:

> - Certainty or Comfort
> - Variety
> - Connection or Love
> - Significance
> - Growth
> - Contribution

Robbin's Six Basic Human Needs intertwine with Maslow's Hierarchy of Needs and McClelland's Need for Achievement Theory.

Certainty or Comfort comes from knowing how things work and how others behave. If you can predict events and actions, you will feel safe, and that will bring comfort. Certainty permits you to learn to trust. Certainty is related to control.

Uncertainty, on a positive note, can add stimulation and create a sense of adventure adding **variety** in your life. However, according to Robert Kail and John Cavanaugh's book, *Human Development: A Lifespan View*, uncertainty in a person's life before the approximate age of six will interfere with that person's confidence to take on adventure.

Without certainty, there will not be stability and safety in which to go forth in life with confidence to achieve security in connection. Fear will interfere with connection.

Connection or Love grows out of bonds and relationships with other people and animals. Without **connection**, life can be lonely; there is little feeling of **significance** or value. Your need for **connection** is related to your sense of identity and need for belonging and affiliation.

Significance in life comes with feeling you have purpose and value in your home growing up as well as in your social and work environments. Significance adds to your esteem, self-actuation, and achievement.

Growth encompasses physical, chronological, educational, professional, and spiritual development. Physical and chronological growth is programed into your cells. On the other hand, educational, professional, and spiritual growth stem from arousal (a stimulation for **variety**), identity development, and the need for achievement.

Contribution means being active, and that increases connection to people, which builds self-esteem, identity, self-actuation, and achievement similar to **significance**. Contribution can be seen by interactions with other people and society at large.

If any of the Six Basic Needs are not being met in a developmental environment, the child's likelihood of achieving high self-esteem, a solid identity, autonomy, and actuation will most likely be compromised.

If your environment did not convey a message of your significance, you may not recognize the contribution you have to offer friends or organizations as you grow and develop. Without the three building blocks of significance, certainty, and connection, your emotional development, achievement, and contribution will be affected.

If your environment was uncertain because a caregiver's behavior was unpredictable, their mood inconsistent, different people were continuously coming and going, caregivers were being changed regularly, or there was violence, abuse, or substance use, then these circumstances would contribute to uncertainty.

Even if a caregiver spends hours tuned into the TV or computer, significance within the child is compromised because a connection or relationship with the caregiver is blocked and validation of their importance is lost.

Negative beliefs are embedded deep within us and are seldom identified or easily understood. The negative beliefs present obstacles to advancement, productivity, functional relationships, enjoyment in life, and happiness. The negative beliefs undermine good health by creating potential stress and anxiety. Negative beliefs are worth investigating.

Triggers

Triggered emotions drive your motives and subsequent behaviors and responses to various situations. Triggers cause you to respond quickly and emotionally to situations. Remember, if you find yourself reacting very strongly to a situation, so strongly that your reaction is far greater than the situation warrants, it is a triggered emotion.

The old feeling being triggered is our body's effort to point it out to our adult Self in an attempt to resolve the old wound by rewriting the end of the story.

Our adult Self needs to take an action or make a decision that will resolve the old hurt or helpless feeling that keeps us stuck and repeating our usual reactionary behavior patterns.

Our self-parenting will demonstrate a new way to communicate or behave in order to gain control and bring resolution—thereby creating a positive memory to store in our hippocampus (chapter 3).

Identifying a triggered emotion, signals a "code blue." Your body is demanding that you bring your equilibrium back into balance. By producing tension in your voice, muscle tension in your body, increased heart rate, perspiration, watering eyes, or a feeling like you just want to run, your body is announcing the presence of stress.

Your awareness needs to call out a whoa command, noting, "Something is out of proportion to the circumstance here," so you can then ask, "How can I redirect and defuse this energy?"

*Out of clutter, find simplicity.
From discord, find harmony.
In the middle of difficulty
lies opportunity.*

—Albert Einstein—

While you may or may not want to attach circumstances to your triggers, what is critical is that you acknowledge that something inside of you is being activated and is crying out in an attempt to get your attention begging you to resolve the present situational unrest and restore equilibrium within your body.

The Comprehensive Plan

It is time to tie together all the many pieces of information that this book has presented. My goal has been to assimilate all of what I have researched and learned into one cohesive holistic package.

Let's review how the 8 strategies come together. At any moment in the day, you can use **Mindfulness—strategy 1** to identify your state of mind.

Mindfulness can also be isolated for use throughout the day just when you feel like taking a two-second break to "let go." It can be used before you go into an important meeting as a way in which to compose yourself or to unwind before turning out your light at night to go to sleep.

Mindfulness creates a wonderful meditative exercise with numerous reported health benefits. Check out the mindfulness information included in the Reframing Exercises and Supplemental Information Packet available for free download: http://bit.ly/ReframeExercise

Visual Imagery—strategy 2 will initiate a reduction in the physiological effects of stress and anxiety. It can be used as soon as you recognize the presence of stress or tension to help clear your mind and prepare yourself to reframe your viewpoint. Visual imagery can also be used by itself to offset panics or phobias without combining it with reframing.

Self-Awareness—strategy 3 will allow you to more fully analyze the dynamics of present situations, thereby allowing you to objectively assess the reality of each one.

Use your emotional climate to disclose which of your Parts is in control—be an investigator of yourself in the present moment.

Insightfulness—strategy 4 will come gradually over time. You can grow from the insights gained; however, reframing your viewpoints is not dependent upon them.

Using the reframing techniques alone will reduce anxiety, but if you have spent time using insightfulness to **See** what is being stirred within, you can more readily formulate the most effective **alternate thought.**

The reframing examples presented throughout this book are only representative of real life but hopefully you have been able to find things in them that you can relate to.

Now that we have gone through many reframing examples, Go back to one of the feelings that were identified in a reframing example that may have resonated with you, such as rejection or not being valued, and revisit it. Return to the feeling and assess whether the reframing example indirectly helped to calm you.

Opening yourself to the emotion being evoked will give it value, and that will initiate the healing process. By listening to your feelings and becoming familiar with them, you value yourself and demonstrate the love and nurturing that perhaps you feel you did not receive when you were young.

This is how to parent yourself and make yourself significant. Most of us determine our significance based on our core story and how others react to us. True significance comes from what *we think of ourselves*—this is what yields peace and this is why it is critically important that you bring resolution to your core story.

*Don't forget to fall in love
with yourself first.*

—Carrie Bradshaw—

Forgiveness—strategy 5 and Empathy—strategy 6 are useful mindsets to employ when connecting to people under every circumstance. They lead to forward movement, compassion, and caring, which nurture all relationships.

Establishing the **Habit—strategy 7** is what will lead to ease, comfort, effectiveness, and the speed at which you move out of your stressful state. Habits will also lead to modifying the reframing techniques to best meet your needs and situations because having the habit means you are using it regularly enabling you to more quickly discern the quickest reframing method for the situation at hand.

We also learned that habits compose our comfort zones and that habits can be modified and changed to serve us better, bring us better health, lead to personal growth, and can be understood to be the obstacles to creating change in our lives.

Risk-taking—strategy 8 is needed for your personal growth. The more frequently you take risks to test old beliefs, experiment to gain new experiences, rewrite your standard method of operation, and stretch yourself to reach new goals, understandings, and changes in your perceptions and outlooks, the sooner life will take on new meaning, excitement, friendships, and adventures.

The **Reframing Technique:** This is the tool promising to transform fear into calm. Using an **alternate thought** will bring a form of resolution to your anxiety and help you to see a way to move forward with energy. Each resolution will provide an example for future episodes of unrest that will demonstrate adult ways in which to navigate life—expanding your resources and providing you with better options for handling anxiety.

You may not be able to discover the reasons for the anxiety right away. Please remember, it may require many sessions of spending time before you gain an insight. Experiencing what you may have felt in the past is a way to begin to work through a feeling and move to a place where your self-parenting can help you to resolve a situation and rewrite the end of your core story.

If understandings seem blocked, please consider seeking professional help. Working through the obstacles will bring you the truth. The truth is what will eventually set you free, and you will see a life beyond what you are afraid of. There is so much waiting for you.

You will begin to see a different future. Often, we cannot parent ourselves until we have been able to explore what happened in our past so that we can learn who we are and understand *how* to nurture ourselves.

Chapter Wrap-up

You have given yourself a gift by reading *Reframe Your Viewpoints* and in this chapter we have summarized the eight stand-alone and supportive strategies in addition to the technique of reframing so that you can start to bring change into your life.

Because of the amount of information in this learning guide, it would be difficult to assimilate everything in one reading and there are many sections of this book that could serve as a resource to you as you implement the reframing habit—both now and in the future.

Your Action Plan

The best way to predict the future is to create it.

—Peter Drucker—

Practice each day. Take daily steps—no step is too small. Focus on *how* you can achieve rather than *why* you can't. Never stop growing. Never give up.

Determine whether you are *interested* in what has been presented in this book or whether you are *committed* to these goals. If you are interested, you will do what is convenient. If you are committed, you will say, "Yes." Your inner game plan determines your outer result. When you say "Yes"—change can occur. When you say, "Yes"—you give yourself Hope! Why live a life dictated by your past?

Set aside a three-month trial period using these techniques as *consistently and earnestly* as possible—not half-heartily. At the end of the trail period, if you have been reframing regularly, you will be able to measure a change in the quality of your life.

Measuring change from day to day does not provide you with enough information to assess. A trail period will provide you with tangible proof of the potential benefit the reframing technique may offer you.

You owe it to yourself—a three-month trial is a tiny commitment when compared to the rest of your life. A three-month trail will provide you with a glimmer of what is possible. Refer back to this book regularly. Each time you read it, a deeper understanding of the information and strategies will be gained and that will add to your efficacy.

In chapter 12, we will look at how you can shape your future, I hand the reins over to you, and we talk about the timeline for change.

Chapter 12

Scale the Wall

*Whatever you're thinking
and feeling today
is creating your future.*

—Paraphrasing of the Law of Attraction—

Where Do You Want to Lead Yourself?

The first step toward change is knowledge and the dream of something different. Change can occur only after you recognize that a different way may exist. With this book you now have a diving platform from which to spring so that you can transform your moments of stress successfully. From that knowledge, a pathway for change will open within you and continue over the years to redefine your existence.

It's a tremendous challenge that I am setting before you. Learning new skills, taking risks, and establishing habits take time and effort in your already-busy life. You may feel reluctant to employ the level of dedication that will be required to create the habits needed to reframe your viewpoints and rewire your brain. This is why it is so important for you to go at your own pace and in your own style to avoid burnout, prevent throwing in the towel, and loosing the possibility for the potential benefits that await you.

*Your thoughts are the architects of
your destiny.*

—David O. McKay—

What Is the Timeline?

Creating change is a gradual process because at the same time you are trying to absorb new information, you are trying to understand the "why" and "how" as well as decipher and believe in the information coming back at you from everything you are implementing.

However far you travel in this journey and to whatever varying degree you ultimately use reframing, I am confident that you will reduce the level of stress in your life to a lower and healthier intensity.

Be sure to allow yourself as much time as it may take. You can break the plan into steps, taking one strategy at a time, getting comfortable with that and using the energy from that accomplishment to move into the next one. Remember, this is not a race—it is an evolution.

The beauty of evolution is that it is a progressive journey that will continue for the rest of your life—you will determine the depth and extent of your evolution by your energy— everyone continues to evolve until the moment they take their last breath. You can choose to float along the river of life or you can choose to paddle with these skills. I believe you are ready to paddle.

The information within this book has awakened in you the concept of understanding yourself from a different perspective. You are reframing who you are.

You are beginning to fathom that becoming a fully integrated individual means you know and understand all of your many identities and love each and every one of them. You understand that that is what will eventually allow peace to reside within your heart and the searching and turmoil can be replaced with confidence.

You are beginning to grasp that change is not about throwing out your traits or self-beliefs. It is about exploring those beliefs, challenging them, and taking the risks in life to disprove their worth—thereby demonstrating to yourself that your old safe rules only harm you and reinforce your childlike decisions. Your rules and self-beliefs remain strong and in place because they have been your lifetime habits.

You can now see how your rules and self-beliefs have been toxic and detrimental to your wellbeing. Your *dedication* to your beliefs has been one of your great strengths and now you can apply that dedication to strengthening new beliefs and beneficial behaviors that will help you to grow and mature and leave behind harmful patterns. We are never done maturing.

Now, you have information and practices that can reshape those self-beliefs and construct the modifications needed to lead yourself forward. You can begin to grow who you are by using your strengths to help you accomplish your goal. Up to now, one of your strengths has been your *dedication* to your old self-beliefs. You are now ready to harness that dedication and lead yourself to your new truth.

Notice, we have just reframed your *dedication* (to old self-beliefs) to be a beneficial strength and important tool to help lead you through your evolution—we did not throw the dedication away because it was misdirected—we redirected it.

In reality, we have awakened in you a new understanding of what you can be. Refer back to and reread the different chapters. Keep all this information circulating through your mind as you traverse your days so that you refresh your purpose. It will take more than being interested; it will take commitment to the changes you are hoping for.

The important thing to remember is that movement will occur incrementally and any gain needs to be celebrated. Daily small steps will lead to full-length strides. You may feel a benefit the first time you reframe, or it may take several practices. That is where dedication and patience are needed to stay the course—I promise they will bring payback.

I encourage you to stay the course because the calm and confidence you can attain will provide you with far-reaching benefits.

There will be stretches in your life where focus and practice on these techniques just do not fit into the busy demands of your day. BUT each time you come back to it, you will build on what you accomplished previously. Nothing will have been wasted.

Discipline is the bridge between
goals and accomplishments.

—Jim Rohn—

Once you start this process, it will build on itself. Once you begin this type of work, it begins to take on a life of its own that perpetuates further understanding and growth. Let the energy of discovery lead the way. Freedom from your internal doubts and control over your angst will be your future reward and enjoyment in life.

Approach this process as part of your life's journey, not as an "if convenient" add-on. Commit to utilizing this plan consistently, and give yourself adequate time to connect to yourself. It will be through that connection that you will experience the deepest peace of all.

Your dedication will strengthen your efficacy, refine your techniques and make using the reframing technique something you incorporate into each day.

I am no different from you. I do not possess any special characteristics or abilities that enabled my establishing new neural pathways and permanently transforming my anxiety into confidence and peace. I did develop unyielding self-awareness.

I took it one day at a time, tapping into the perseverance and diligence I have referred to throughout the book. I am a no more disciplined person than you—I was committed to myself, through learning and self-parenting, and I trusted in the process of self-growth. I continue on my journey every day receiving renewed energy from every step I continue to take.

Through the consistent use of reframing and the 8 strategies, especially risk-taking, I have *become* a disciplined person. If we have to help our inner child Parts to grow up, then we should think about the timeline for that progression from a parenting perspective.

Parenting children takes years, why should we expect parenting ourselves to take any less time. Parenting our inner child means giving it time, patience, love, and understanding—not criticism, judgment, or impatience.

We all have many different Parts inside and each Part needs our acceptance—we cannot throw Parts of ourselves away but we can remodel them so that we can become a more functionally integrated person.

What Can We Expect to Control?

Parenting and guiding yourself along this new path will bring you a sustained sense of fulfillment and ultimately, will put control over the pursuit of your inner peace into your hands. Providing the stability, understanding, love and leadership that your "multitudes" (inner children) are seeking will bring them peace. When all your Parts have been recognized and heard, and you are using reframing and risk-taking regularly, resolution, confidence, and fulfillment will become your reward.

The misconception and belief that you will attain comfort and peace if and when you can control your *environments* creates the opposite outcome. A need for control over your environments *causes* inner turmoil and pain because consistently controlling our environments is not possible. It is your *inner* control that will bring your peace and calm.

The only potential control you can hope to possess in life is what you hold in your mind and maintain in your attitude, because you have no control over others or what they are thinking. Therefore, cultivate the integration and awareness of all aspects of who you are—leading to certainty in your heart. The integration and love of your "multitudes" will set you free to confidently handle the inevitable twists and turns in life as comfortably as possible.

> *You have control over three things:*
> *what you think; what you say;*
> *and how you behave.*
> *To make a change in life, you must*
> *recognize these gifts are the most*
> *powerful tools you possess*
> *in shaping the form of your life.*
>
> —Sonya Friedman—

Sensing Change

As you experience success with these strategies, please understand that time is needed to establish them as habits, and that reliable and frequent use of those habits will require a very conscious effort on your part for quite a while.

Measuring your progress, in my view, should be assessed on nothing shorter than a six-month period of time. However, the three-month trial will reflect some level of change.

Progress will be seen on different levels. Baby steps are progress. After six months of working at your own pace, ask yourself some of the following questions. If you can answer, "Yes" or recognize an increase in frequency to any one or more of these questions, then you will have made progress.

> Are you using mindfulness more regularly during your days?

> Are you finding regular moments for self-discovery through awareness as compared to before the purchase of this book?

> How much risk-taking are you purposefully inserting into your days?

> Have you had positive results from your experimentation?

> How quickly are you now aware of stress hijacking your body?

> Are you regularly inserting cleansing breaths into your day?

> Does the thought of reframing a situation enter your mind as an option?

> Are you using reframing more now after a couple of months than when you first finished reading this book?

> Do you understand your inner dynamics any better today than you did before you began reading *Reframe Your Viewpoints*?

Throughout the creating change process, I would consider feelings of inadequacy or questioning whether it is all just too difficult might be expected.

If that occurs, use these **alternate thoughts** if you encounter those emotions:

> I will be patient with my evolution;

> Reframing my life is an evolutionary process—evolutions do not have timelines or particular achievement points;

> They are what they are—there is no predetermined level of accomplishment—there are too many factors involved;

> I am where I am in my evolution and I will be at this stage until I am ready to move on to the next one.

At The Center of Success

Awarenesss is the **first step** needed in driving your success and it is at the center of all that you dream of changing. Nothing can be changed without your awareness of the need for change or the awareness of when it is time to make a different choice.

Increasing your skills in objective awareness will help to move you closer to your goals more quickly. The self-awareness of *when* you are in a child "Part," will be your most significant accomplishment toward self-understanding.

You need to align the conscious and the non-conscious thinking processes. Strive to be in Self as consistently as possible.

Acceptance of all that you discover is the **second step** in your change process. Allowing yourself to own your Parts, accept them as friends who need adult guidance, and accept that those Parts have imperfections and vulnerabilities that can be redirected over time.

Perfection is not something humanly achievable. Acceptance of your imperfections and allowing yourself to not be perfect will eliminate your need to wear an outer mask—allowing you to be authentic. That alone will carry you far in your goal to reduce internal tension and achieve inner peace.

Step three, loving and liking yourself with all your imperfections, past mistakes, and regrets is your ultimate goal and that will bring you the deep and lasting peace you desire. Having compassion and empathy toward yourself will open you to self-love. Change is waiting for you.

Reframing can change your entire reaction-to-life landscape! If you find you are having success transforming anxiety into peace—spread the word, recommend this book, and share what you have learned.

We all deserve to live in confidence. If many readers become aware of reframing as a new life-management skill, it may constitute a positive shift in society toward more peace in general and true connection between each other. Don't keep this valuable tool to yourself—share it.

Your commitment to reframing will open the possibility for a different type of life. That is exactly what I want for you! It would be my pleasure to hear from you if you have questions or comments. Perhaps there is another aspect of this process that I have not addressed—how can I be of help to you? Consider a complimentary coaching session and experience the transforming energy coaching offers. https://www.CreatingChangeLifeCoaching.com/complementary-session.html

FIND YOUR HEART, CONNECT TO IT, AND LISTEN

*You are never too old
to set another goal
or to dream a new dream . . .*

—C. S. Lewis—

BELIEVE IN WHAT
YOU CAN BECOME
www.theultimatequotes.in

References

Barber, Dan (2016). *Parenting from prison: 5 lessons from kids behind bars* [Kindle version]. Retrieved from http://www.amazon.com

Bourne, E. J. (2002). *The Anxiety and phobia workbook* (3rd ed.). Oakland, CA: New Harbinger Publications.

Chessid, Davina (2016). *Food crazy mind: 5 simple steps to stop mindless eating and start a healthier, happier relationship with food* [Kindle version]. Retrieved from http://www.amazon.com

Dispenza, Joe (2007). *Evolve your brain: The science of changing your mind.* Deerfield Beach, FL: Health Communications, Inc.

Doidge, Norman (2007). *The brain that changes itself: Stories of personal triumph from the frontiers of brain science.* New York, NY: Penguin Books.

Glasser, William (1999). *Choice theory: A new psychology of personal freedom.* New York, NY: HarperCollins.

Goulding, Regina A., & Schwartz, Richard C. (1995). *The mosaic mind: Empowering the tormented selves of child abuse survivors.* Oak Park, IL: Trailheads Publications.

Hanh, Thich Nhat (2007). *The art of power.* New York, NY: HarperCollins.

Howard, Sethanne, & Crandall, Mark W. (Fall 2007). Post traumatic stress disorder: What happens in the brain? *Journal of the Washington Academy of Sciences, 93*(3) 14.

Kail, Robert V., & Cavanaugh, John C. (2002). *Human development: A lifespan view.* Belmont, CA: Wadsworth/ Thomson Learning.

Klettke, Otakara (2016). *Hear your body whisper: How to unlock your self-healing mechanisms* [Kindle version]. Retrieved from http://www.amazon.com

Ogden, Pat, Kekuni, M., & Pain, Clare (2006). *Trauma and the body: A sensorimotor approach to psychotherapy.* New York, NY: W. W. Norton and Company.

Price, Sara Elliott (2014). *Mindfulness for beginners: How to use mindfulness to find peace and happiness living in the present moment* [Kindle version]. Retrieved from http:// www.amazon.com

Schwartz, Richard C. (1995). *Internal family systems therapy.* New York, NY: Guilford Press.

Schwartz, Richard, C. (2008*). You are the one you have been waiting for: Bringing courageous love to intimate relationship*s. Oak Park, IL: Trailheads Publications.

Simon, S. B., & Simon, S. (1990). *Forgiveness: How to make peace with your past and get on with your life.* New York, NY: Warner Books, Inc.

Spiegler, M. D., & Guevremont, D. C. (2010). *Contemporary behavior therapy* (5th ed.). Belmont, CA: Wadsworth.

Talbot, Shawn (2002). *The cortisol connection: Why stress makes you fat and ruins your health—and what you can do about it.* Berkeley, CA: Hunter House.

About the Author

Virginia has a desire to help people stretch and grow in how they navigate life. Virginia believes peoples' in-the-moment choices will lead them to their desires and goals. Combining information and incentive sets the stage for their choosing to create change that can lead them toward attaining their desired wishes.

Virginia chose to explore why fear, obsessive thinking, body image dissatisfaction, generalized discomfort in life, and depression plagued her. Through personal research and courageously stretching herself beyond what she had accepted as her lot in life, Virginia has attained a life almost free from the oppression with which she once lived. She hopes to provide hope for others around the world.

Virginia and her husband have two grown children and three grandchildren. They reside in Orlando, Florida, and share a life rich in family interactions both in Orlando and in their travels to Bogotá, Colombia, where their daughter works, to spend time, visit and share connection with that family.

Before You Go

Thank you for reading *Reframe Your Viewpoints*. I realize you have thousands of books to browse and choose from when buying a book—the fact that you selected this book deeply rewards me. I hope this book has added insights and momentum to your quest to achieve more peace and confidence in your life.

YOU CAN HELP! Your opinion is very important, as is my goal of making reframing a household word so that more and more people can learn and benefit from the reframing technique. Help me share this information with your friends and connections on social media.

I look forward to your feedback and ask that if you have found this book interesting and helpful, you consider leaving an honest review for Reframe Your Viewpoints by clicking on the Amazon link below. A one-to-three sentence review is like gold to the author and potential reader.

http://smarturl.it/ritterbusch-reframe

I wish you great success as you move forward in your goals.

Sincerely,
Virginia Ritterbusch

Post Script

If writing a book is or ever has been a glimmer in your eye, I encourage you to click on the link for Self-Publishing School presented below. It will offer information to you that may begin to take you on another journey. Life should be full of journeys that add variety into your life.

NOW IT'S YOUR TURN

Discover the EXACT 3-step blueprint you need to become a bestselling author.

Self-Publishing School helped me, and they can help you with this FREE VIDEO SERIES!

Even if you're busy, bad at writing, or don't know where to start, you CAN write a bestseller.

With tools and experience across a variety of niches and professions, Self-Publishing School is the only resource you need to take your book to the finish line!

Watch this VIDEO SERIES to become a bestselling author:

https://xe172.isrefer.com/go/curcust/rittervl

Made in the USA
San Bernardino, CA
11 January 2019